D1764743

The National Archives and Records Administration

KNOW YOUR GOVERNMENT

The National Archives and Records Administration

Christina Rudy Smith

CHELSEA HOUSE PUBLISHERS

Chelsea House Publishers
Editor-in-Chief: Nancy Toff
Executive Editor: Remmel T. Nunn
Managing Editor: Karyn Gullen Browne
Copy Chief: Juliann Barbato
Picture Editor: Adrian G. Allen
Art Director: Maria Epes
Manufacturing Manager: Gerald Levine

Know Your Government
Senior Editor: Kathy Kuhtz

Staff for THE NATIONAL ARCHIVES AND RECORDS ADMINISTRATION
Assistant Editor: James M. Cornelius
Copy Editor: Nicole Bowen
Deputy Copy Chief: Ellen Scordato
Editorial Assistant: Elizabeth Nix
Picture Researchers: Michele Brisson and Mark Galan
Assistant Art Director: Laurie Jewell
Senior Designer: Noreen M. Lamb
Production Coordinator: Joseph Romano

First Printing

1 3 5 7 9 8 6 4 2

Library of Congress Cataloging-in-Publication Data
Smith, Christina Rudy.
    The National Archives and Records Administration.
    (Know your government)
    Bibliography: p.
    Includes index.
    1. United States. National Archives—Juvenile literature. 2. United States. National Ar-
chives and Records Administration—Juvenile literature. I. Title. II. Series: Know your gov-
ernment (New York, N.Y.)
CD3023.S65 1989   025.17′14′0973   88-29965
ISBN 1-55546-073-9
      0-7910-0868-1 (pbk.)

CONTENTS

KNOW YOUR GOVERNMENT

CHELSEA HOUSE PUBLISHERS

INTRODUCTION

Government: Crises of Confidence

Arthur M. Schlesinger, jr.

From the start, Americans have regarded their government with a mixture of reliance and mistrust. The men who founded the republic did not doubt the indispensability of government. "If men were angels," observed the 51st Federalist Paper, "no government would be necessary." But men are not angels. Because human beings are subject to wicked as well as to noble impulses, government was deemed essential to assure freedom and order.

At the same time, the American revolutionaries knew that government could also become a source of injury and oppression. The men who gathered in Philadelphia in 1787 to write the Constitution therefore had two purposes in mind. They wanted to establish a strong central authority and to limit that central authority's capacity to abuse its power.

To prevent the abuse of power, the Founding Fathers wrote two basic principles into the new Constitution. The principle of federalism divided power between the state governments and the central authority. The principle of the separation of powers subdivided the central authority itself into three branches—the executive, the legislative, and the judiciary—so that "each may be a check on the other." The *Know Your Government* series focuses on the major executive departments and agencies in these branches of the federal government.

The Constitution did not plan the executive branch in any detail. After vesting the executive power in the president, it assumed the existence of "executive departments" without specifying what these departments should be. Congress began defining their functions in 1789 by creating the Departments of State, Treasury, and War. The secretaries in charge of these departments made up President Washington's first cabinet. Congress also provided for a legal officer, and President Washington soon invited the attorney general, as he was called, to attend cabinet meetings. As need required, Congress created more executive departments.

Setting up the cabinet was only the first step in organizing the American state. With almost no guidance from the Constitution, President Washington, seconded by Alexander Hamilton, his brilliant secretary of the treasury, equipped the infant republic with a working administrative structure. The Federalists believed in both executive energy and executive accountability and set high standards for public appointments. The Jeffersonian opposition had less faith in strong government and preferred local government to the central authority. But when Jefferson himself became president in 1801, although he set out to change the direction of policy, he found no reason to alter the framework the Federalists had erected.

By 1801 there were about 3,000 federal civilian employees in a nation of a little more than 5 million people. Growth in territory and population steadily enlarged national responsibilities. Thirty years later, when Jackson was president, there were more than 11,000 government workers in a nation of 13 million. The federal establishment was increasing at a faster rate than the population.

Jackson's presidency brought significant changes in the federal service. He believed that the executive branch contained too many officials who saw their jobs as "species of property" and as "a means of promoting individual interest." Against the idea of a permanent service based on life tenure, Jackson argued for the periodic redistribution of federal offices, contending that this was the democratic way and that official duties could be made "so plain and simple that men of intelligence may readily qualify themselves for their performance." He called this policy rotation-in-office. His opponents called it the spoils system.

In fact, partisan legend exaggerated the extent of Jackson's removals. More than 80 percent of federal officeholders retained their jobs. Jackson discharged no larger a proportion of government workers than Jefferson had done a generation earlier. But the rise in these years of mass political parties gave federal patronage new importance as a means of building the party and of rewarding activists. Jackson's successors were less restrained in the distribu-

tion of spoils. As the federal establishment grew—to nearly 40,000 by 1861—
the politicization of the public service excited increasing concern.

After the Civil War the spoils system became a major political issue.
High-minded men condemned it as the root of all political evil. The spoilsmen,
said the British commentator James Bryce, "have distorted and depraved the
mechanism of politics." Patronage, by giving jobs to unqualified, incompetent,
and dishonest persons, lowered the standards of public service and nourished
corrupt political machines. Office-seekers pursued presidents and cabinet
secretaries without mercy. "Patronage," said Ulysses S. Grant after his
presidency, "is the bane of the presidential office." "Every time I appoint
someone to office," said another political leader, "I make a hundred enemies
and one ingrate." George William Curtis, the president of the National Civil
Service Reform League, summed up the indictment. He said,

> The theory which perverts public trusts into party spoils, making public
> employment dependent upon personal favor and not on proved merit,
> necessarily ruins the self-respect of public employees, destroys the
> function of party in a republic, prostitutes elections into a desperate
> strife for personal profit, and degrades the national character by lower-
> ing the moral tone and standard of the country.

The object of civil service reform was to promote efficiency and honesty in
the public service and to bring about the ethical regeneration of public life. Over
bitter opposition from politicians, the reformers in 1883 passed the Pendleton
Act, establishing a bipartisan Civil Service Commission, competitive examina-
tions, and appointment on merit. The Pendleton Act also gave the president
authority to extend by executive order the number of "classified" jobs—that is,
jobs subject to the merit system. The act applied initially only to about 14,000
of the more than 100,000 federal positions. But by the end of the 19th century
40 percent of federal jobs had moved into the classified category.

Civil service reform was in part a response to the growing complexity of
American life. As society grew more organized and problems more technical,
official duties were no longer so plain and simple that any person of intelligence
could perform them. In public service, as in other areas, the all-round man was
yielding ground to the expert, the amateur to the professional. The excesses
of the spoils system thus provoked the counter-ideal of scientific public administration, separate from politics and, as far as possible, insulated against it.

The cult of the expert, however, had its own excesses. The idea that
administration could be divorced from policy was an illusion. And in the realm
of policy, the expert, however much segregated from partisan politics, can

never attain perfect objectivity. He remains the prisoner of his own set of values. It is these values rather than technical expertise that determine fundamental judgments of public policy. To turn over such judgments to experts, moreover, would be to abandon democracy itself; for in a democracy final decisions must be made by the people and their elected representatives. "The business of the expert," the British political scientist Harold Laski rightly said, "is to be on tap and not on top."

Politics, however, were deeply ingrained in American folkways. This meant intermittent tension between the presidential government, elected every four years by the people, and the permanent government, which saw presidents come and go while it went on forever. Sometimes the permanent government knew better than its political masters; sometimes it opposed or sabotaged valuable new initiatives. In the end a strong president with effective cabinet secretaries could make the permanent government responsive to presidential purpose, but it was often an exasperating struggle.

The struggle within the executive branch was less important, however, than the growing impatience with bureaucracy in society as a whole. The 20th century saw a considerable expansion of the federal establishment. The Great Depression and the New Deal led the national government to take on a variety of new responsibilities. The New Deal extended the federal regulatory apparatus. By 1940, in a nation of 130 million people, the number of federal workers for the first time passed the 1 million mark. The Second World War brought federal civilian employment to 3.8 million in 1945. With peace, the federal establishment declined to around 2 million by 1950. Then growth resumed, reaching 2.8 million by the 1980s.

The New Deal years saw rising criticism of "big government" and "bureau-cracy." Businessmen resented federal regulation. Conservatives worried about the impact of paternalistic government on individual self-reliance, on community responsibility, and on economic and personal freedom. The nation in effect renewed the old debate between Hamilton and Jefferson in the early republic, although with an ironic exchange of positions. For the Hamiltonian constituency, the "rich and well-born," once the advocate of affirmative government, now condemned government intervention, while the Jeffersonian constituency, the plain people, once the advocate of a weak central government and of states' rights, now favored government intervention.

In the 1980s, with the presidency of Ronald Reagan, the debate has burst out with unusual intensity. According to conservatives, government interven-tion abridges liberty, stifles enterprise, and is inefficient, wasteful, and arbitrary. It disturbs the harmony of the self-adjusting market and creates worse troubles than it solves. Get government off our backs, according to the popular cliché, and our problems will solve themselves. When government is necessary, let it be at the local level, close to the people. Above all, stop the inexorable growth of the federal government.

In fact, for all the talk about the "swollen" and "bloated" bureaucracy, the federal establishment has not been growing as inexorably as many Americans seem to believe. In 1949, it consisted of 2.1 million people. Thirty years later, while the country had grown by 70 million, the federal force had grown only by 750,000. Federal workers were a smaller percentage of the population in 1985 than they were in 1955—or in 1940. The federal establishment, in short, has not kept pace with population growth. Moreover, national defense and the postal service account for 60 percent of federal employment.

Why then the widespread idea about the remorseless growth of government? It is partly because in the 1960s the national government assumed new and intrusive functions: affirmative action in civil rights, environmental protection, safety and health in the workplace, community organization, legal aid to the poor. Although this enlargement of the federal regulatory role was accompanied by marked growth in the size of government on all levels, the expansion has taken place primarily in state and local government. Whereas the federal force increased by only 27 percent in the 30 years after 1950, the state and local government force increased by an astonishing 212 percent.

Despite the statistics, the conviction flourishes in some minds that the national government is a steadily growing behemoth swallowing up the liberties of the people. The foes of Washington prefer local government, feeling it is closer to the people and therefore allegedly more responsive to popular needs. Obviously there is a great deal to be said for settling local questions locally. But local government is characteristically the government of the locally powerful. Historically, the way the locally powerless have won their human and constitutional rights has often been through appeal to the national government. The national government has vindicated racial justice against local bigotry, defended the Bill of Rights against local vigilantism, and protected natural resources against local greed. It has civilized industry and secured the rights of labor organizations. Had the states' rights creed prevailed, there would perhaps still be slavery in the United States.

The national authority, far from diminishing the individual, has given most Americans more personal dignity and liberty than ever before. The individual freedoms destroyed by the increase in national authority have been in the main the freedom to deny black Americans their rights as citizens; the freedom to put small children to work in mills and immigrants in sweatshops; the freedom to pay starvation wages, require barbarous working hours, and permit squalid working conditions; the freedom to deceive in the sale of goods and securities; the freedom to pollute the environment—all freedoms that, one supposes, a civilized nation can readily do without.

"Statements are made," said President John F. Kennedy in 1963, "labelling the Federal Government an outsider, an intruder, an adversary. . . . The United States Government is not a stranger or not an enemy. It is the people of fifty states joining in a national effort. . . . Only a great national effort by a great people working together can explore the mysteries of space, harvest the products at the bottom of the ocean, and mobilize the human, natural, and material resources of our lands."

So an old debate continues. However, Americans are of two minds. When pollsters ask large, spacious questions—Do you think government has become too involved in your lives? Do you think government should stop regulating business?—a sizable majority opposes big government. But when asked specific questions about the practical work of government—Do you favor social security? unemployment compensation? Medicare? health and safety standards in factories? environmental protection? government guarantee of jobs for everyone seeking employment? price and wage controls when inflation threatens?—a sizable majority approves of intervention.

In general, Americans do not want less government. What they want is more efficient government. They want government to do a better job. For a time in the 1970s, with Vietnam and Watergate, Americans lost confidence in the national government. In 1964, more than three-quarters of those polled had thought the national government could be trusted to do right most of the time. By 1980 only one-quarter was prepared to offer such trust. But by 1984 trust in the federal government to manage national affairs had climbed back to 45 percent.

Bureaucracy is a term of abuse. But it is impossible to run any large organization, whether public or private, without a bureaucracy's division of labor and hierarchy of authority. And we live in a world of large organizations. Without bureaucracy modern society would collapse. The problem is not to abolish bureaucracy, but to make it flexible, efficient, and capable of innovation.

Two hundred years after the drafting of the Constitution, Americans still regard government with a mixture of reliance and mistrust—a good combination. Mistrust is the best way to keep government reliable. Informed criticism is the means of correcting governmental inefficiency, incompetence, and arbitrariness; that is, of best enabling government to play its essential role. For without government, we cannot attain the goals of the Founding Fathers. Without an understanding of government, we cannot have the informed criticism that makes government do the job right. It is the duty of every American citizen to know our government—which is what this series is all about.

The Louisiana Purchase Treaty was signed in 1803 by Emperor Napoleon Bonaparte of France and President Thomas Jefferson when Napoleon sold the Louisiana Territory to the United States to help fund his European wars. The National Archives safeguards historic documents such as this treaty.

ONE

Preserving America's Past

On one occasion she mounted a mule and rode to the Federal camp in the night-time and notified them of a threatened attack by the rebels."

Although Margaret A. Dement lived in the South during the Civil War, she did not support the Confederacy. Because she and her family remained loyal to the Union, they were threatened by their neighbors and suffered for their loyalty. One night, despite the danger, she rode alone through the dark to warn Union soldiers of an attack planned by Confederate soldiers. How do historians know about Mrs. Dement's bravery? Her story is preserved in the records of the National Archives.

The National Archives of the United States contains a record of its country's past that is unequaled anywhere in the world. In the case of Margaret Dement, whose activities illustrate a small part of the Civil War, the past was preserved by the House of Representatives. The Archives has authority to mine the legislative branch as well as hundreds of government agencies for records vital to our national history. After the Civil War, the federal government created the Southern Claims Commission. It helped Southerners whose property had been confiscated by the Union army if they could prove they had remained loyal to the Union even while living in the South. The stories found in these claim files offer a surprising glimpse into the lives of Americans and how they were affected by the Civil War. So into the National Archives these files went.

Amended **PETITION.**

To the Honorable Commissioners of Claims,

Under the Act of Congress of March 3, 1871, Washington, D. C.:

The Petition of (1) *Margaret A. Dement*

respectfully represents:

That (2) *a* citizen of the United States, and resident at present at or near (3) *Jenkins Ferry Grant Co. Ark.*

and that (4) he resided when this claim accrued at or near (3) *Jenkins Ferry*

That (5) the has (6) a claim against the United States for property (4) *Taken*

for the use of the army of the United States during the late rebellion at (or near) *Jenkins Ferry*, in the county of *Grant*, and State of *Arkansas*.

That the said claim, stated by items, and excluding any and all items of damage, destruction, and loss, (and not use,) of property; of unauthorized or unnecessary depredations by troops and other persons upon property, or of rent or compensation for the use or occupation of buildings, grounds, or other real estate, is as follows:

No. of Item	QUANTITIES AND ARTICLES.	VALUE.	
1	6 Head cattle weighing 400 lbs each 2400 lbs @ 5¢ per lb	126	
2	400 lbs Bacon 20¢ per lb	80	
3	200 Bushels corn @ $1 per Bushel	200	
4	3000 Rails at $10 per 100	30	
5	3000 feet pine lumber at $20 per 1000	60	
6	Carpenter tools	25	
7	9 Yearlings (calves) at $8 per head	72	
8	2 Calves at $5 each	10	
9	30 Bushels Wheat $2 per Bush	60	
	Total,	657	

Note 1. Give full names of all the petitioners.
2. Give the evidence of each petitioner.
3. Give the former residence of each petitioner.
4. "Taken," or "furnished."

After the Civil War, southerners loyal to the Union, such as Margaret Dement, petitioned the Southern Claims Commission for compensation for property confiscated during the war. Petitions, census records, and other public documents at the National Archives allow a glimpse into the lives of past generations of Americans.

What the Archives Contains

Many people are surprised to learn that stories about the everyday lives of ordinary Americans can be found in the National Archives. They expect to find only the important state papers of the U.S. government. And, indeed, those documents are there. The Declaration of Independence, the Constitution, and the Bill of Rights are permanently displayed in the rotunda of the National Archives. Treaties between the United States and foreign governments are preserved in the National Archives: In 1804 President Thomas Jefferson and French emperor Napoleon Bonaparte signed a treaty that added the enormous Louisiana Territory to U.S. lands. Now the Louisiana Purchase Treaty lies safely in a vault with other treaties.

Other state papers are also kept in the National Archives. Presidential proclamations are preserved, including the Emancipation Proclamation, which President Abraham Lincoln signed to free the South's slaves on New Year's Day, 1863. Congress's declaration of war against Germany in 1917 is there. Another state paper, the only one of its kind, can be found in the National Archives—Richard Nixon's 1974 letter of resignation as president of the United States, which he sent to the secretary of state.

The records of federal courts—the Supreme Court, district courts, appeals courts, and claims courts—are housed in the Archives or in one of its 11 field branches around the country. And the enormously important work of the legislative branch of the federal government, including congressional staff committees and watchdog agencies—the General Accounting Office, for example—and all of the legislation proposed each year in Washington, is kept in its own Center for Legislative Archives within the National Archives.

The significance of treaties, presidential proclamations, and other state papers is obvious. Most people recognize that they should be saved perma-

---

THE WHITE HOUSE
WASHINGTON

August 9, 1974

Dear Mr. Secretary:

I hereby resign the Office of President of the United States.

Sincerely,

Richard Nixon

The Honorable Henry A. Kissinger
The Secretary of State
Washington, D.C. 20520

President Richard M. Nixon's concise letter of resignation is part of the National Archives' permanent collection.

nently. However, the National Archives also saves certain kinds of routine government paperwork that may not bear a president's signature or mark any milestone in American history. To an archivist, the value of a record is not always determined by who signed it. A record is considered valuable if it documents the organization, policies, or activities of the U.S. government or if it contains information necessary for researchers. For instance, the records that describe how astronauts were chosen for the first Apollo flights of the 1960s may not have a famous signature, but they explain an important development in the space program. These and other records in the National Archives—the famous documents and the routine paperwork—tell the story of America's people and their heritage.

Why We Need a National Archives

Before the National Archives was established in 1934, this documentary heritage was in danger of being lost. Each federal agency was responsible for protecting its own outdated papers, and some agencies were better guardians

Prior to the establishment of the National Archives, it was up to each government agency to maintain its own files. The War Department files, pictured here in the White House garage, early in the 20th century, illustrate the perilous conditions to which most records were exposed.

than others—some stored their work everywhere from the back room to basements, garages, attics, and other unsuitable places where the documents were vulnerable to fire, insects, mold, and water.

Government workers were concerned about the fate of these records. Others, especially historians, eventually became alarmed and began to lobby Congress, urging it to act in the interest of the nation's documentary heritage. In the early 1920s, when several fires destroyed valuable historical records, the American Legion also joined the fight to protect the records. Formed after World War I to protect the interests of war veterans, the American Legion was particularly concerned about the fate of military-service records. It used its considerable political influence to help fight for a national archives that would provide good care for the fighting man's records.

In 1926, Congress finally responded to public pressure by authorizing construction of the first building to house the government's records. In 1934 it took the next logical step by creating an agency, the National Archives, to care for these precious records within the new building. Today the headquarters of the National Archives is still its original, neoclassical building on Constitution Avenue, just off the Capitol Mall, in Washington, D.C.

The agency has expanded over the years to become a national network of 11 field branches, 14 records centers, and 9 presidential libraries and museums. Professional archivists, now working throughout the country, help federal agencies manage their records, decide which records are valuable and merit preservation, and determine which records can be destroyed, choosing the right time for their destruction.

After the documents are formally placed in one of the National Archives buildings across the country, archivists provide a safe environment for them to ensure that they last for future generations. Reference archivists confer with researchers and help guide them to those records most useful for their work.

Who Uses the Archives?

Who uses these records so carefully preserved in the National Archives? Historians do, certainly, but many nonscholars also come to use the records— most people who come to the Archives are doing genealogical or family-history research, because the Archives has a wealth of information for helping to trace a family's lineage. Much of this data comes from the U.S. Census Bureau, which every 10 years takes a meticulous census, or count, of American citizens. Genealogists use the census records to learn who lived where, when, and with whom. They can also use passenger-arrival lists in the National Archives to prove when an immigrant arrived in the United States.

Buttons, Bibles, and Vietnam

Military-service records can provide valuable and sometimes intimate information about a person by documenting his or her service record; the records may also, if the spouse or children applied for benefits, give information about a veteran's family. (Some birth, marriage, and death certificates are also stored in the National Archives, though most remain in town halls and other local repositories.)

In the case of revolutionary war veterans, applying for a pension was especially difficult. As a result, a search of those military-service files can reveal some particularly strange items. The War Department did not create or preserve a service record for every man who fought, so applicants had to give proof of service in the militia or Continental army and of the length of their service. Widows and children also had to prove that they were related to the veteran. As proof of kinship, relatives occasionally sent in love letters, or the family bible, which often contained names, birth dates, or other family information. And to prove military service, one family submitted an invitation the veteran had received to dine with General George Washington during the war. Another family sent buttons from the coat the veteran wore in battle. Because the War Department did not return these keepsakes to the pension applicants, the files now in the National Archives contain more than papers for the genealogists and historians to ponder.

Other researchers find different uses for the records in the National Archives. Workers in federal agencies depend on the agency to retrieve old files needed again for current business. Lawyers often research the records to establish the rights of their clients; sometimes their client is the federal government, other times it is a citizen making a claim against the government. People applying for job-related benefits, such as employment compensation or retirement pay, may use the government personnel records in the Archives. Preserving records for their legal value, in fact, is just as important to the stability of the government as it is to scholarship.

It is not just words that are preserved. The Soil Conservation Service, the U.S. Geological Survey, and other agencies have used aerial photography to study and map the land; these aerial photographs are now used by environmentalists who trace changes in land use or by other people trying to settle

FAMILY-REGISTER,
of Mr Nathaniel & Mrs. Mary Bangs.
Mr. Bangs was born October 2, 1760.
Mrs. Bangs was born March 25, 1763.
Were Married January 23, 1783.
By the Revd Josiah Deany of Berry.

Two Children, viz.	Born.	Died.
Isaac H. Bangs	Nov. 23, 1783.	
A Son	Aug. 6, 1785	Aug. 6, 1785.

Mrs. Bangs Died June 29, 1786.

Mr. Bangs was married (by the Revd David Parsons of Amherst) to Miss Electa Kellogg his 2d Wife Jany 15, 1789. She was born August 6, 1764.

Children's names.	Born.	Died.
A Daughter	March 12, 1790.	March 12, 1790.
Mary	May 21, 1791.	
Adolphus	Sep. 21, 1792.	
Sarah	June 8, 1794.	
Electa	Dec. 6, 1795.	
Nathaniel jr.	July 15, 1797.	Nov. 21, 1821.
Joel	Aug. 23, 1802.	

Mr. Bangs   Mrs. Bangs

Naked as from the earth we came And crept to life at first.

We to the earth return again And mingle with our dust.

Mary Adams Maiden-name.   J. Forbes scripsit.

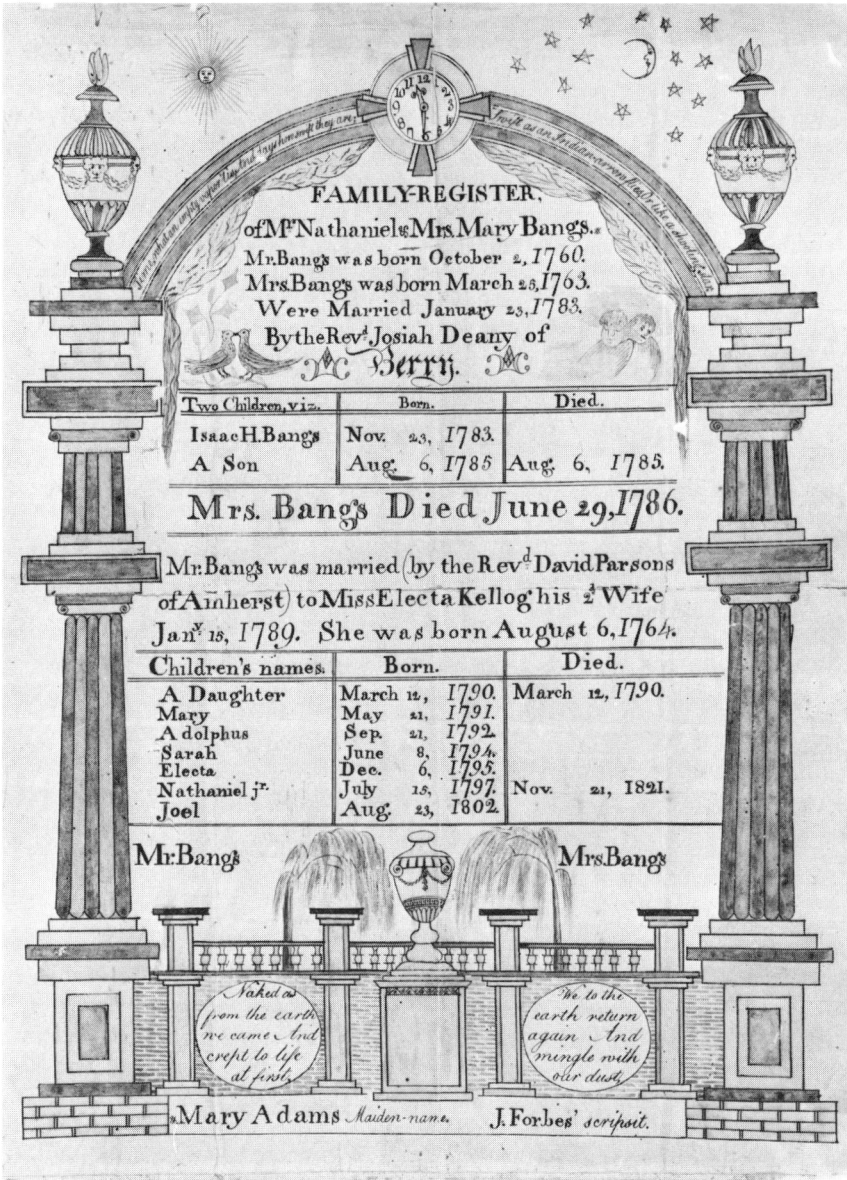

After the revolutionary war some soldiers' families had difficulty proving that they were eligible for a military pension. To establish a relationship to a veteran, widows and children might use a love letter, a Bible, or—as the Bangses did—a family register.

21

The National Archives's collection of architectural drawings, including this one of the post office in Scranton, Pennsylvania, are used by architectural historians and preservationists to accurately restore old buildings.

boundary disputes. Many of the plans used by the federal government in building hundreds of post offices, lighthouses, and offices across the country are housed in the National Archives. Even model shipbuilders make their way to the Archives's door: They can find plans for hundreds of ships built for the navy since the revolutionary war.

People throughout the country benefit from research in the Archives, though they may never use the records themselves. Architectural historians and preservationists use the records to trace different building styles and help city planners save the best buildings from the past. Tourists delight in visiting historic sites and museums where the displays may be based on the curator's research at the National Archives. Biographers, novelists, and movie and television screenwriters sometimes use the records in the National Archives—on period costumes, American Indians, railroad depots, patents, paper money, newspaper layout, the extent of electrification—to make their books and shows more accurate and enjoyable.

The records of the federal government, both the important state papers and the more mundane paperwork, offer a firsthand look into the past. Preserving these records, in whatever form, ensures that a vivid picture of American history will always be available.

The Constitution of the United States, the foundation of American democracy, is on permanent display in the rotunda of the National Archives building.

TWO

The Fight for a National Archives

In the spring of 1776, American colonists were on the verge of war against England. For years, they had protested the actions of King George III and the English Parliament, hoping for a restoration of the liberties taken from them. But protests had not worked and; in fact, England had retaliated by levying additional taxes and placing more constraints on American liberties. The Continental Congress decided there was no hope for reconciliation with England and voted to declare independence. On July 4, 1776, it adopted the Declaration of Independence, a statement explaining to the world the colonists' reasons for rebellion.

The Declaration of Independence and other papers of the colonial leaders were organized and protected by Charles Thomson, secretary of the Continental Congress. At its first meeting in September 1774, the Continental Congress appointed him secretary because the members believed their proceedings should be preserved for posterity. The early leaders had a fine awareness of the magnitude of their political experiment, and they took pains that few leaders have since. One archivist of this century has written that "no one could have been a more careful record-keeper than Charles Thomson . . . and no one more solicitous for the safety and preservation of these prized records than George Washington." Today, the documents they safeguarded, including the Declaration of Independence, are found in the National Archives.

Charles Thomson, appointed secretary of the First Continental Congress in 1774, carefully recorded its proceedings for posterity.

The young nation's third president, Thomas Jefferson, also expressed concern about the safekeeping of the country's important papers. In 1801 he wrote to Secretary of State James Madison that he was sending his official papers to the State Department because he had "no confidence that the office of the private secretary of the U.S. will ever be a regular & safe deposit for public papers." As a result of Jefferson's caution, his letter is now safely filed in the Archives among the records of the Department of State.

The First Steps

America's bold beginning as a republic inspired other nations with the dream of government by people rather than by kings, and in 1789 the French people overthrew their monarch, Louis XVI. France's new government quickly set up what is considered the world's first national archives, and other nations drew from that example. As early as 1810, the U.S. government officially recognized the problem of preserving its record of the past when Congress appointed a committee to "Inquire Into the State of the Ancient Public Records and Archives." As a result of this investigation, Congress passed the first act meant to provide improved storage for the government's papers. Signed by President James Madison on April 28, 1810, it was the first step in the very long process of establishing a national archives.

During the War of 1812, the British attacked Washington, D.C., the country's new capital. Clerks in the State Department rescued many documents that might have been lost by hiring wagons and horses to take the records to safety just days before the battle. They moved the Declaration of Independence and other documents first to an unused gristmill about two miles from the city. By August 24, 1814, while the British were burning many government buildings, the Declaration rested in safe storage at Leesburg, Virginia, about 35 miles northwest of the capital.

In spite of these sometimes heroic efforts by government officials to save the nation's documents, the natural enemies of paper—fire, insects, heat, water, and sunlight—did much damage. Fire, especially, can be catastrophic.

British soldiers burned much of Washington, D.C., including the Capitol, shown here, in 1814. Fortunately, federal clerks saved many important documents from destruction—including the Declaration of Independence—by moving them to Leesburg, Virginia.

Because of careless storage, the Supreme Court's landmark decision in Marbury vs. Madison, *written by Chief Justice John Marshall in 1803, is partially burned. That case established the judicial branch's preeminence in the government, giving it the power to set aside any statute of Congress that it considers unconstitutional.*

A major fire destroyed the Treasury building in March 1833. In December 1836, another one broke out in the building occupied by the Post Office and the Patent Office. Although few books and papers of the Post Office were destroyed, the Patent Office lost many valuable models and papers. Fire was far more common in an era of wooden floors, open hearths, and candlelight, but it took the double loss of these two fires to prod Congress into action. Plans for a new Patent Office building were already under way when the second fire occurred. To prevent any more losses, Congress authorized construction of new fireproof buildings for the Treasury Department and the Post Office.

In 1877 catastrophe again prompted government officials to consider how best to protect the records, when a major fire at the Interior Department destroyed many valuable papers. In reaction, Quartermaster General of the Army Montgomery C. Meigs designed a hall of records. It was perhaps the first design for a building that could protect all of the government's older records and gather them in one place.

In addition to the damage done by the fire, the problem of safely housing the government's records grew worse during the 19th century. In the nation's first 70 years, from 1789 to 1860, the government accumulated about 108,000 cubic feet of records. As the nation and its government grew exponentially over the next 55 years, from 1860 to 1916, another 923,000 cubic feet of records were added.

Politicians and Historians Team Up

Throughout these first 100-odd years, attempts to preserve the important papers of the government came primarily from government officials. They concentrated their efforts on finding a safe place to keep the out-of-date papers and on protecting them from fire, water, insects, and other threats. The sudden growth in the number of records during and after the Civil War greatly increased officials' concern about the lack of suitable storage space. Some officials suggested building fireproof rooms in different agencies. Quartermaster Meigs had suggested and designed a hall of records where the papers from all agencies would be stored together, but not until other parties outside the government got involved, in the late 19th and early 20th centuries, was the fate of the records addressed.

One of these new voices began to be heard in the late 19th century when American universities first granted graduate degrees in history. The new professional historians from these graduate schools depended on the preser-

29

vation of original records to do research. After the American Historical Association (AHA), a new organization of professional historians, was founded in 1884, it took the lead in the fight.

J. Franklin Jameson (1859–1937) was foremost among the historians who fought for the creation of a national archives. Jameson received one of the first doctoral degrees in history granted by an American university, Johns Hopkins University, in Baltimore, Maryland, in 1882. After earning his doctorate, he taught for several years at Johns Hopkins, Brown University, and the University of Chicago. He left Chicago in 1905 to become director of the Bureau of Historical Research at the Carnegie Institution, in Washington, D.C., where he stayed until 1928. He then became head of the Manuscripts Division of the Library of Congress. Jameson was a founder of the AHA and throughout his career worked to advance the interests of professional historians. While in Washington, he frequently lobbied congressmen to gain support for concerns of the historical community.

Interest in history was not confined to schools at this time. Attention to

J. Franklin Jameson, one of the first recipients of an American doctoral degree in history, fought hard for the founding of a national archives.

history is a mark of every major civilization, which is what the United States was becoming after the Civil War, and the public knew it. Some of the nation's first great works of history were appearing: Francis Parkman's chronicles of western exploration and of the French and Indian wars; George Bancroft's 40-year project, *History of the United States;* Henry Adams's studies of the early years of the Republic and how they prepared the way for growth. The nation's centennial of independence, in 1876, also added fuel to the public feeling that theirs was a story worth telling and preserving.

Jameson's Campaign

It was in this cultural setting that Jameson urged the AHA, in 1895, to speak up for the preservation of documentary materials. In response, the AHA created its Historical Manuscripts Commission and named Jameson as chairman. Only four years later, the AHA realized that the records of the government itself were the papers deserving the most attention, so it created the Public Archives Commission. In 1901, at the urging of the latter commission, the AHA endorsed the building of a hall of records in Washington.

Federal records are important, and Jameson and other historians gradually realized that a hall of records, which would merely protect the documents, was inadequate. He began to distinguish between a hall of records and a national archives. His goal became the establishment of the latter.

The difference between a hall of records and an archives is critical. Both are safe places to store records. But in a hall of records every agency would control its own records; agency officials would be free to keep or destroy as many or as few records as they pleased. One agency could choose to keep every scrap of paper it created, costing the taxpayer useless maintenance and storage. Another agency could choose to destroy nearly every file it created, losing that information forever. In contrast, an archives would not only store records safely, but a staff of professional archivists would be trained to decide which records to keep and which to destroy. All the records of the many government agencies would be administered equally and fairly.

Jameson was assisted in encouraging the construction of a national archives by Waldo G. Leland, who worked for him at the Carnegie Institution. Leland was recognized as an authority in the developing field of archival science after he and Claude H. Van Tyne published their *Guide to the Archives of the Government of the United States in Washington* in 1904. This survey helped alert historians to the need for federal archives. Leland also helped develop and publicize many of the theories of archival science. Jameson used his associate's ideas about the principles to be followed and the type of building and organization that could best do the job to persuade members of Congress to support a national archives.

The efforts of Jameson and Leland led the AHA to resolve, in 1910, that Congress should move forward with construction. Jameson followed up by urging that Congress create the agency itself as well. Correctly thinking that most people would be more impressed by marble and granite than by the papers housed therein, his tactic was first to urge the building of an archives and later to worry about developing the organization to fill it.

In 1913 it appeared that Jameson was successful when President William Howard Taft signed a bill that authorized planning for a federal archives building, including $5,000 for preliminary architectural plans. The bill also provided for visits to and inspections of archives buildings in Europe. In August 1914 President Woodrow Wilson signed the necessary appropriations bill.

Snags in the Plan

Unfortunately, the plan soon ran into problems. The Department of the Treasury decided that $5,000 was not enough money for preliminary plans and did not start work until 1915, when a new staff reversed the decision. By then World War I had begun, and the European inspection trips became impossible. Deleting the provision for transatlantic study required new legislation, causing further delay.

During World War I, preoccupation with the war prevented Congress and the president from taking any more steps on the matter. Once the war was over, in 1918, pressure to create a federal archives began to build again. In January 1921 a fire destroyed nearly all the census records of 1890, the most extensive one undertaken to that time. In the wake of this incalculable loss, many newspapers took up the cause for the safe storage of records and increased the pressure on Congress to act quickly before any more were destroyed.

Perhaps the most significant step toward Jameson's goal also occurred in the 1920s, when the politically powerful American Legion gave its support to the cause. After World War I, veterans formed the American Legion to advocate their concerns. The organization was primarily meant to help veterans resume civilian life and to assist widows, children, and disabled veterans. In addition,

it wanted to promote memorials to honor the war dead and to oversee the care given to service records of veterans. In 1921, led by its national historian, Eben Putnam, the Legion called for the construction of a building to house all national archives, including military-service records. Working closely with Jameson and Leland over the next few years, Putnam acted as point man in the Legion members' push for an archives.

Advancing to the Goal

Public sentiment was on the Legion's side, as it had been for the historians two decades before. American nationalism surged in the 1920s on the strength of the war victory and a booming economy and, more darkly, in the form of tight restrictions placed on immigration. But the public's general agreement on an issue is not always enough to spur Congress into action. In spite of the increased public pressure after the 1921 fire and from the American Legion, Congress did not authorize construction of a national archives until 1926. Many congressmen refused to support any building projects in Washington until additional construction of federal buildings across the country was approved. So a bill had to be passed that included regional construction as well as construction of a national archives in the capital. President Calvin Coolidge signed the bill on May 25, 1926. By July, Congress passed actual appropriations for it.

On February 19, 1933, President Herbert Hoover (left) laid the cornerstone for the National Archives building.

A drawing of the Mall in Washington, D.C. Designers proposed various locations for the National Archives, but the winning site (center) was chosen because it is midway between the White House (left) and the Capitol (right).

Progress was fast thereafter. In 1930 the Treasury Department, then responsible for the construction of federal buildings, selected John Russell Pope as architect. (Pope was also the architect of the National Gallery of Art and the Jefferson Memorial, both completed in 1937.) Ground was broken in 1931, and on February 20, 1933, in the last two weeks of his presidency, Herbert Hoover laid the cornerstone.

With the first part of Jameson's goal in the works—the building—the second part began to take shape, and he was instrumental in pushing through the legislation that established the agency itself. The bill was introduced in Congress in 1934, and, with some personal attention from President Franklin D. Roosevelt, it was quickly passed that same year. Finally, the National Archives was ready to begin its job.

Stacks, or storage areas, at the National Archives. Archival filing systems, unlike those of libraries, keep records in the order in which they were created and group them according to their creating agency.

THREE

Growth and Change

The early 1930s were hard years for America. With millions of people out of work during the depression, President Roosevelt and Congress were obliged to start many new programs to help the economy recover and put people to work. Known collectively as the New Deal, these programs included the Civilian Conservation Corps (CCC), which gave young men jobs improving the environment by planting trees, fighting fires, and building parks. In another program, the National Recovery Administration (NRA) asked industry to govern itself by writing codes for businesses to follow. The Works Projects Administration (WPA) put the unemployed to work on public projects such as school buildings, flood control, sewage treatment plants, and reforestation. One WPA program paid unemployed artists, musicians, and writers for such public-minded activities as painting murals in post offices and writing states' histories.

Preoccupied with the press of New Deal programs, Congress was not quick to pass a law establishing the new agency of the National Archives. However, as the building neared completion, Congress began to consider what powers it should give the new agency. Some believed that the archives should include only the most valuable, landmark documents of American history; others thought the new agency should also control all older records of the government.

During the depression, employees of the Works Projects Administration flatten and smooth documents to better preserve them for safe-keeping at the Archives.

And if the archives cared for all older records, should the agency be given the authority to dispose of valueless papers? Congress also considered whether to make the archives independent or to include it in an existing government agency, perhaps the Library of Congress or the National Park Service.

Getting off the Ground

By early June 1934, Congress settled these questions and passed an "Act to establish a National Archives of the United States Government." The legislation made the National Archives an independent agency headed by the archivist of the United States, who would be appointed by the president. The archivist was given responsibility for all records belonging to the government of the United States. The act gave him the power to inspect the records of the government wherever they were stored, to transfer them to the National Archives, and to make regulations for their care and use after they were housed. He was also given the power, with the approval of Congress, to dispose of records with no permanent value or historical interest.

The act also allowed the archivist to appoint people to his staff without regard to civil-service laws, which required applicants for government jobs to take a competitive exam. Exemption from these regulations left the first archivist free to define the qualifications and responsibilities of the new profession. Because there was only a very small pool of working archivists in this country, the first archivist hired people with graduate degrees in history.

In addition, the legislation included two extra provisions. First, the National Historical Publications Commission (NHPC) was created to encourage the publication of historical documents across the country. A separate organization, the NHPC was linked to the Archives through its chairman, who was to be the archivist of the United States. J. Franklin Jameson, who had led the fight for an archives, again used his influence to effect this provision.

The other unusual provision authorized the National Archives to accept, store, and preserve motion-picture films and sound recordings that pertain to American history. This provision allowed the Archives to add privately produced films to its collection of those made by government agencies.

The First Archivist

As President Roosevelt considered whom to appoint as the first archivist of the United States, the AHA suggested Robert D. W. Connor, professor of history at the University of North Carolina. Connor had served as secretary of the North Carolina Historical Commission, where he developed the state's Department of Archives and History. Historians regarded him highly as an archivist and administrator and as a fellow historian. President Roosevelt agreed, and on October 10, 1934, he announced the appointment of Connor as first archivist of the United States.

Connor assumed his new duties almost immediately. Because the National Archives building was not yet completed, he started to work in offices in the Justice Department building, across the street. The new staff he hired turned

Along with his staff, Robert D. W. Connor, appointed the first archivist of the United States in 1934, undertook the enormous task of finding, sorting, and organizing federal records, which at the time were scattered around the Washington area.

39

its attention to defining exactly how the new building would be used, and before construction was finished, they recommended several changes. The most significant went to the heart and soul of an archives' function—they requested more *stack areas,* the large rooms full of metal shelves for storing documents. A large interior courtyard had been planned for the building, but to provide more storage for documents, this courtyard was filled in with stacks.

Connor needed to know how many records were still to be brought into the National Archives. Using the authority given to him in the National Archives Act to "inspect personally or by deputy the records of any agency of the United States Government," Connor sent deputy examiners to every government agency. By reviewing the old or inactive files, the archivists could plan the growth and work of the new agency.

For five years the deputy examiners searched for records stored in Washington and its suburbs. They found old records, many of them damaged

The National Archives building under construction in 1934. Architect John Russell Pope designed the neoclassical building, which was completed the next year.

Craftsmen complete the sculpting work on the capitals for the National Archives building.

by fire, water, and rodents, kept in such places as basements, garages, abandoned buildings, and attics. They opened file drawers and boxes to estimate the number of documents they found and to take down vital information about them. During this first survey, the number of records found and considered valuable exceeded all previous estimates. Even with additional stack areas built in the interior courtyard, the volume of records would fill two-thirds of the stacks. Archivists were alarmed by the huge number, and they feared they would rapidly run out of space. Indeed, whereas the government had accumulated about 1.5 million cubic feet of records between the Civil War and World War I, in the 1930s it was producing a million cubic feet every year, according to one historian.

Besides locating and transferring the important old records, the archivists also started to destroy those records that were not worth saving. The National Archives Act required the archivist to give Congress an annual list of those records that had no permanent value and could be destroyed. Government agencies sent lists of inactive records to the National Archives, where special examiners reviewed the lists and recommended whether to keep or destroy

The Archives's staff began its search for old government files in 1934. It found many records, including these film reels in the Department of the Navy, carelessly stored and completely disorganized.

the papers. Their work eventually led to the development of record schedules that allowed routine paperwork with no permanent value to be disposed of at regular intervals.

The search completed and the building finished, the next task was to make the records available for research. Archivists wanted federal agencies and the public to know about the records and how to use them.

To organize the records in such a way that this enormous body of information would be accessible, archivists relied on two important archival principles learned from older European archives.

Archival Methods

The first principle, called *provenance* (which means source), prescribes that a group of records created by one organization should not be mixed with the records of another organization. For instance, the Department of Agriculture has files about cattle ranches in Texas. The Environmental Protection Agency (EPA) might have studied the same region and also have files about it. But archivists would not combine the two files even if the contents were related. Department of Agriculture records remain together, separate from the records of every other department or agency. This principle can seem a burden to a student delving into territorial expansion in the West, for instance, because some data will be stored under the army, some in the maps collection, some with the Interior Department, and so forth. But this principle ensures that the records from one source will never get lost within those from another.

According to the second important archival principle, known as *original order*, the archivist should keep records in the same order as they were filed by their creator. For example, from 1910 to 1944, the Department of State used a decimal filing system for its central files. Basically, the system divided correspondence into nine major subjects, such as extradition and matters concerning commerce, customs administration, and trade agreements, each designated by a decimal code. Following the principle of original order, an archivist would not reorganize the files under new subject headings, as in a reference library, even in the hope of improving the filing system.

Early members of the Archives staff knew and respected the principles of provenance and original order. Their challenge was to apply these principles to the enormous number of records being created by government agencies. They developed the system of *record groups,* an innovation that allowed them to divide the work into manageable units.

Typically, a record group contains the records of a bureau of an executive agency, such as the Bureau of the Census, or of some comparable unit in the

Employees of the Repair and Preservation division fumigate records of the Veterans Administration in 1936. Some of the records destined for the Archives in the 1930s were ridden with insects, dust, and mold.

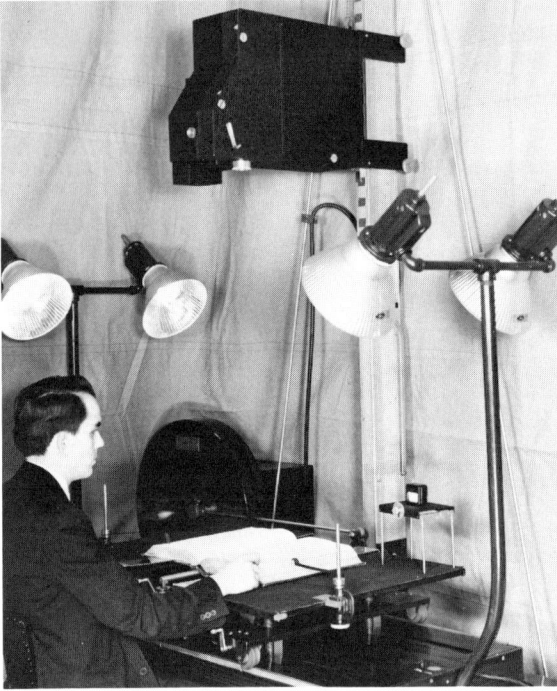

*A microfilm techni-
cian photographs a
valuable manu-
script. The introduc-
tion of microfilming
ensured the protec-
tion of original doc-
uments from wear
and tear.*

government hierarchy. Unlike books in a library, records are not arranged by subject. Different series of records, maintained in their original order, are grouped together according to their link with an agency. For instance, those created by the Veterans Administration became Record Group 15. Some record groups vary a bit from this standard, but all maintain the records in their original order. Organizing the Archives this way made access easier for both staffer and researcher.

As the deputy examiners had discovered, the number of records needing storage in the National Archives greatly exceeded all expectations. So the National Archives began to explore possible uses of *microfilm*. A photographic process, microfilm can reproduce hundreds of pages of documents on a single roll of film. Other repositories had already begun to microfilm records to save space, and microphotography could be put to use in a variety of ways for the National Archives. If a document itself had no intrinsic value that required it to be saved in its original state (in other words, if the Archives wanted to save the information, but not necessarily the paper itself), the record could be microfilmed, the original destroyed.

On the other hand, if a document itself was valuable and deserved preservation, and if it was used often by researchers, it could be microfilmed and put safely into storage. Researchers then used the microfilm, saving the original from wear and tear. Sometimes researchers request reproductions of the same document again and again, so instead of photographing it every time, the National Archives began to retain a negative microfilm copy of such a popular record. They used the negative to make reproductions quickly and easily, avoiding unnecessary handling of the document. During World War II, microfilm was considered an important tool for security work. Valuable records could be microfilmed and, as a precaution, the duplicate copy stored separately.

Publications and Libraries

In the agency's early years, as Connor and his staff were busy surveying the records and setting up systems to handle them, Congress gave them an additional responsibility. Only one year after the National Archives Act was

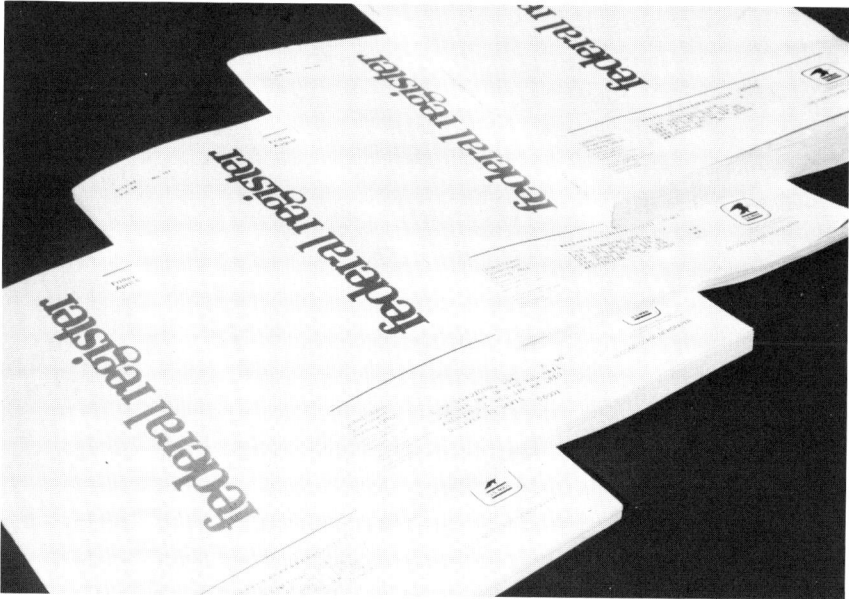

The Federal Register, *published daily by the National Archives, informs the public of regulations issued by the executive branch. It also contains presidential proclamations and executive orders.*

passed, Congress passed the Federal Register Act. It made the National Archives responsible for issuing the *Federal Register,* a daily publication that informs the public about changes and proposed changes in the rules and regulations of the agencies in the government's executive branch. The Archives benefited from this new task in two ways. As the archivist contacted the people at every agency who were responsible for sending new regulations to the Federal Register Division for publication, he built a valuable network of contacts for the Archives—he and his agency became part of the government community, not merely its repository. Additionally, the Archives was certain to get copies of these important documents from all agencies for its own files.

According to the act, the *Federal Register* should contain "any presidential proclamation or executive order and any order, regulation, rule, certificate, code of fair competition, license, notice, or similar instrument issued, prescribed, or promulgated" from an executive agency. The first issue was published in March 1936. Government agencies, attorneys whose work involved the federal government, and others who needed to know their rights and responsibilities as set out by federal agencies immediately recognized its value. Within a few years, the Federal Register Division was also given responsibility to issue the *Code of Federal Regulations,* an annual publication that lists all current regulations of executive-branch agencies and that incorporates the changes listed in the daily *Federal Register.*

The role of caretaker also came to the National Archives in these early years when it assumed control of the Franklin D. Roosevelt Library. The acquisition eventually led to the establishment of the presidential library system, which is now an important part of the National Archives. Aside from his long career in political life, Roosevelt was interested in history and was proud of being the one to have signed the National Archives Act into law. He knew the study of history depended on the availability of materials for research, so he wanted the papers from his entire career to be kept together, maintained in good condition, and made available to researchers. He decided to give his papers to the nation and build a library for them on his estate in Hyde Park, New York. He asked an advisory committee of prominent historians to help plan the library. The committee included Dr. Connor, Waldo G. Leland, and a historian from Harvard University, Samuel Eliot Morison.

In 1939 both houses of Congress authorized the archivist to accept the gift of President Roosevelt's papers, as well as the library building and the land it was on. The National Archives was to preserve the papers and, most important, to make them available to researchers.

By virtue of his varied and lengthy career, Roosevelt's papers are among the

The Franklin D. Roosevelt Library in Hyde Park, New York, was President Roosevelt's gift to the National Archives in 1939, along with papers from all periods of his life.

most interesting of any American official's. In his capacity as assistant secretary of the navy, he helped draft a new constitution for the Caribbean nation of Haiti after the fall of its government in 1915. As New York's governor in the depression years of 1929–33, he set up programs to help the unemployed as "a matter of social duty." During World War II he kept up a huge correspondence with Prime Minister Winston Churchill of Great Britain and met several times with Churchill, Soviet premier Joseph Stalin, and other world leaders. His personal life bears notice, too—he battled polio in middle age, and his wife, Eleanor, was a dynamic and intelligent social activist. Evidence of all phases of FDR's life are found at the library in Hyde Park.

Roosevelt's decision to give his papers to the nation set an important precedent. Many earlier presidents had taken their papers with them when they left office. As a result, the fate of their papers was uncertain, and many were lost, destroyed, or scattered. The two presidents who immediately followed Roosevelt, Harry S. Truman and Dwight D. Eisenhower, both gave their papers to the nation. The National Archives took custody and makes them, too, available to the public.

What was becoming a tradition soon became law when Congress passed the Presidential Libraries Act of 1955, during Eisenhower's first administration. Thereafter the National Archives would have the authority to accept the papers

47

and other historical materials of the presidents, as well as land and buildings, donated by ex-presidents or private citizens, to make a whole system of presidential libraries.

The World War II Years

In the early 1940s the National Archives had to cope, like everyone else, with the many changes wrought by World War II. A pressing concern throughout the government was how to control the enormous number of records created during the war. The Archives helped by quickly taking in a greater number of inactive files from other agencies, which freed up valuable space in the agencies for more offices and workers.

The war brought other changes to the Archives. When the flagship building had opened in 1934, several stack areas were outfitted with specially crafted steel containers to hold the documents. But steel was vital to the war effort from 1942 to 1945, so archivists developed new cardboard containers to be used in stack areas not yet equipped with the steel kind. To many archivists, this change was a blessing because the sharp edges of the steel containers occasionally cut hands or clothing. The new cardboard containers were also lighter and easier to use, and they soon became standard equipment for archives throughout the country.

During the war, the National Archives lost nearly half its staff as people entered military service or left for war work. The remaining staff made war-related work its priority. Archivists quickly processed records from World War I so agencies could learn how wartime problems had been handled then. Archivists found maps and charts in their cartographic and still-photography collections that gave the army, navy, and the Office of Strategic Services (OSS, the precursor to the Central Intelligence Agency) helpful information about the waters and terrain of battle areas.

Like much else about the federal government and America itself during the war, the scope of the Archives's work expanded with the national effort. It began to help agencies improve their record-keeping practices, in a form of assistance called records management. To save the agencies from being overwhelmed by mounting paperwork and to ensure that important records are preserved, records management tackles the entire life of a record, from its creation and use to its final disposition. The object is not merely to minimize paperwork: The Archives hopes to ensure that all agencies create enough records to adequately document their activities, a service to agency managers as well as to future researchers. Then, that need fulfilled, the Archives assists agencies in setting up disposition schedules so that routine paperwork that is valueless for future research can be systematically destroyed when no longer useful. Archives staff members are temporarily reassigned as records officers in other agencies to help out as needed.

The General Services Administration

Success in records management led to another important chapter in the Archives's history. After World War II, Congress was searching for ways to streamline the government. Early in 1949 it began to discuss creating a new organization to oversee construction, maintain buildings, order supplies, and take care of similar administrative concerns for all government agencies. When Wayne C. Grover, then archivist of the United States, learned that Congress might include his agency as part of the new organization, he fought the proposed move. To him and most of the staff, the National Archives was a cultural agency, like the Smithsonian Institution or the Fine Arts Commission, not a machine for keeping everyone's files in order. However, the Archives's

In 1949 Wayne C. Grover, archivist of the United States, led the battle against a congressional proposal to place the National Archives under the jurisdiction of the General Services Administration, which wanted the archivists' skill in records management to be available to all agencies. Grover and his supporters lost the fight.

very success was its undoing. Its expertise in records management convinced Congress that the Archives should be part of the new agency. Congress created the General Services Administration (GSA), and on July 1, 1949, the National Archives became part of GSA.

Not only was the Archives itself (now renamed the National Archives and Records Service, or NARS) placed under the umbrella of GSA; the archivist was also made subordinate. When Congress passed the Federal Records Act in September 1950, it gave the administrator of GSA nearly all the records-management and archival authority previously held by the archivist of the United States, and added some new responsibilities. The act charged GSA with improving standards for the creation, maintenance, and disposition of records throughout the government. In addition, GSA was authorized to operate records centers throughout the country. The change was more in name than in function, for almost immediately the administrator delegated these responsibilities right back to the archivist.

Many archivists were concerned about the loss of independence in NARS. Some feared that their cultural and historical responsibilities as guardians of the nation's historical documents would be overshadowed by the new emphasis on records management. Others were concerned that, because the administrator of GSA was not a professional archivist, he or she might be swayed by political pressure to make unwise choices about daily workings, especially the destruction of sensitive papers. There was also the problem of size—the Archives represented only about 10 percent of GSA's total employees, leaving it vulnerable to being lost in the shuffle.

As the National Archives began to face the challenge of its new status within GSA, the organization was led by Wayne C. Grover, archivist from 1948 to 1965. Unlike his predecessors, he was not a historian. He held a Ph.D. degree in public administration from American University and had been a leader in the field of records management. He was, in other words, the first professional archivist in his post, and he used the new authority given by the Federal Records Act of 1950 to begin improving records management throughout the government.

New Goals Under GSA

The goal of the records-management program was to reduce the number of records and to make those that were preserved more useful and less expensive to maintain. To this end, the Archives began an education program for federal employees, instructing them on what kinds of records should document their agencies' activities and how to maintain those files. In the course of this work, archivists discovered that federal agencies were storing unused records in more than 200 separate locations across the country, at great expense to the government. So the National Archives offered low-cost, centralized storage in its records centers.

The National Historical Publications Commission (NHPC), part of the Archives since its inception, had lain dormant for years when Congress ignored its early recommendations. In the 1940s, the urgency of the war effort also prevented the Archives from supporting the commission's work. But the Federal Records Act of 1950 gave new life to the NHPC by mandating that it "cooperate with and encourage appropriate federal, state, and local agencies and nongovernmental institutions, societies, and individuals in . . . editing and publishing the papers of outstanding citizens of the United States and such other documents as may be important for an understanding and appreciation of the history of the United States." In the past, the commission was headed by a managing secretary who also served as director of publications for the National Archives (the chief archivist had served as ceremonial head); now it would have its own executive director and other staff.

The commission's task was to begin at the beginning: Its first projects were to encourage the publication of the papers of Benjamin Franklin, John Adams, James Madison, John Quincy Adams, Alexander Hamilton, and Thomas Jefferson. At the same time it would direct the publication of documentary histories of the ratification of the Constitution and Bill of Rights and the work of the first federal Congress. By giving its advice and assistance, its prestigious endorsement, and its aid in the search for private financial support, the commission would be fulfilling the ideals of J. Franklin Jameson: It would help to ease the work of researchers studying America's early history.

During Grover's tenure as archivist of the United States, the agency increased its role in records management in the federal government, gained the Hoover, Truman, and Eisenhower presidential libraries in addition to the Franklin D. Roosevelt library, and oversaw an increase in publications by the Federal Register Division and an expansion of the work of the NHPC. In the early 1960s, with the work load growing, Grover found it increasingly difficult to lead his agency while under the management of GSA. The GSA administrators were interested in economy, efficiency, and measurable productivity, but many of NARS's cultural and historical programs, such as reference service and preservation of historical documents, are difficult to measure in those terms. With some frustration, after 17 years as archivist of the United States,

Robert H. Bahmer succeeded Grover as archivist of the United States in 1965. Bahmer introduced projects, such as the journal Prologue, *aimed at increasing the American public's awareness of the Archives's holdings.*

Grover decided to retire in 1965. When he informed President Lyndon B. Johnson of his decision, he repeated the call that the National Archives be made an independent agency once again, and after his retirement he continued to campaign for that cause.

The next archivist of the United States, Robert H. Bahmer, had served as Grover's deputy for those same 17 years. When he became archivist, he was 61 years old. Although he planned to retire soon, he first wanted to start some new programs in NARS. Bahmer believed that archives were of interest not only to historians but also to political scientists, genealogists, economists, and other scholars. He wanted to help the agency reach out to a wider audience.

One project along that line was the launching of *Prologue: Journal of the National Archives.* The journal's goal is to publicize the resources and programs of the National Archives. Published quarterly, it contains a list of records that have recently been *accessioned,* or accepted for legal custody. Its other main feature is historical articles based on records in the National Archives. Recent issues have spotlighted such topics as first ladies of the modern era and the bicentennial of the Constitution. In 1985 one article described a surprising collection of baseball cards in the records of the National Archives—they had been submitted as evidence in a legal case heard by the Federal Trade Commission in 1962.

Another program that expanded the National Archives's constituency is the National Audiovisual Center, established in 1969. It is the central depository for all audiovisual programs produced by the federal government. The center offers for sale or rental more than 2,800 titles in videotape, film, slide/tape, and audiotape formats. Topics include public health, foreign-language instruction, and military training. The center has proved to be a popular and valuable outlet of government work.

Bahmer retired as archivist in 1968, and his successor, James B. Rhoads, continued the quest for new users of the Archives's resources. Rhoads revived the exhibits program at the Archives and encouraged the development of traveling exhibits that could be seen across the country. Though these new programs succeeded, the Archives soon got its greatest boost in the number of researchers from an event archivists did not plan. In 1977 the television

The National Audiovisual Center, established at the Archives in 1969, houses all of the audiovisual programs made by the federal government. The center's staff, shown here checking some film, sell and rent films, videotapes, and slides on a variety of subjects including military training, public health, and foreign-language instruction.

53

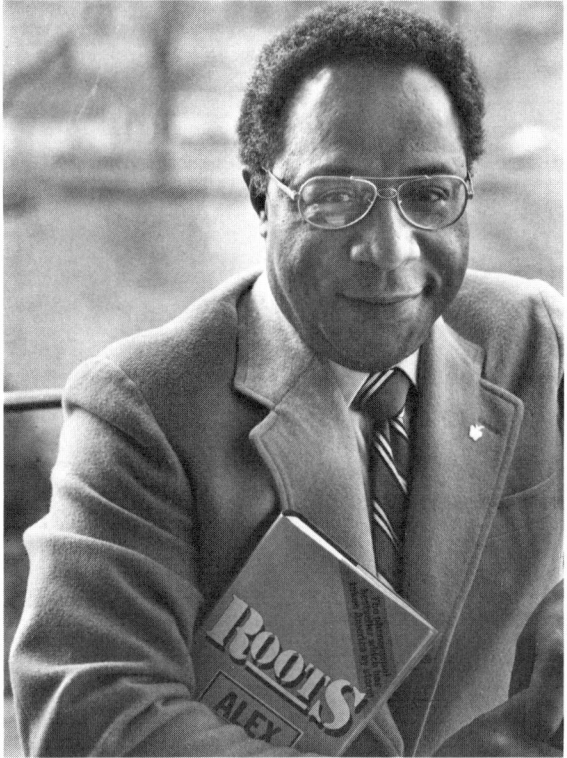

After the miniseries based on Alex Haley's book Roots *was televised in 1977, hundreds of Americans flocked to the National Archives to discover their own family's past.*

miniseries "Roots," based on Alex Haley's book about the history of his family, sparked enormous interest in family-history research. Professional genealogists had long used the records in the National Archives, but after "Roots" amateur family historians also discovered the value of these records, and they besieged every respository from old village halls to the Archives itself on Constitution Avenue. For the first time ever, the microfilm reading room there had waiting lines. Calls, letters, and visits increased, and the amazed staff looked for new ways to help their visitors.

New Freedoms, New Rules

While popular interest in the National Archives was growing, archivists found themselves following new rules concerning access. The Archives had long advocated open access to its records to allow researchers the greatest use of them. In the 1960s and 1970s, the political atmosphere in the country supported more openness in government. In 1966, Congress passed the Freedom of Information Act (FOIA), and in 1974 it passed amendments that put more teeth into the original act. The FOIA was designed to make information gathered or created by the federal government readily available to citizens. In other words, government documents could not be arbitrarily restricted by archivists or by the agency that created them. The FOIA allows agencies to restrict records only if the information in them falls into one of nine categories specified in the act. One category is trade secrets or financial information; another is most records compiled during an investigation by a law-enforcement agency, such as the FBI. There are other categories, including, of course, records classified to protect national security.

Security Issues

National-security information is classified under criteria established by an executive order signed by the president to protect the United States and its citizens and allies. Only people who have received security clearances from the government may see this information. However, so that information will not be withheld from the public unnecessarily, the National Archives systematically reviews all classified records more than 30 years old. Using guidelines from the agency that originally classified the information, archivists and technicians who have security clearance review records to determine if they may be opened to the public. If a record contains information that is still sensitive, it is withheld from researchers. It will not be made available to the public until it is reviewed again and ultimately declassified.

The goal of the Freedom of Information Act and of this systematic review of classified documents is to make records available to researchers as soon as possible. Yet soon after Congress encouraged these goals by passing forceful amendments to the FOIA, it also passed the Privacy Act of 1974, which allows the restriction of records with information of a highly personal nature about a living person. Working with these two conflicting pieces of legislation, archivists are challenged to balance an individual's need for privacy against a researcher's need for information.

The issue of access to records became especially sensitive during the administration of President Richard M. Nixon. Many members of Congress believed his administration misused its authority and wrongly restricted access to records. One attempt by President Nixon to restrict access was especially controversial and caused many to question whether the National Archives belonged in GSA.

President Nixon resigned in August 1974 because of his role in what came to be known as the Watergate affair. Officials in the White House had been linked to a burglary of the Democratic party's national campaign headquarters at the Watergate office complex in Washington, D.C., before the 1972 election. During the congressional investigation of the scandal, a White House staff member revealed that President Nixon had tape-recorded thousands of conversations held in the Oval Office. Congress subpoenaed the tapes, which later confirmed that the president tried to cover up his complicity in the crime. Having lost the support of Congress and the public and facing the threat of impeachment, President Nixon resigned, the first president ever to do so.

Shortly after he resigned, Nixon signed a controversial agreement with the

Placing politics ahead of history, Arthur Sampson, administrator of the GSA, and former president Richard M. Nixon struck a deal in 1974 to destroy tapes of Nixon's Oval Office conversations and to restrict public access to his presidential papers. Congress, however, quickly passed legislation that prevented the tapes' destruction and allowed access to the materials.

administrator of GSA, Arthur F. Sampson, concerning his papers and the infamous tapes. The agreement limited access to many of his papers to an extraordinary degree and arranged for the destruction of the tapes. In the past, the head of GSA had always consulted with the archivist before signing such agreements. This time, however, Sampson, who had been active in Republican politics in Pennsylvania before joining GSA, failed to consult the archivist. This omission alerted many Americans to the danger of allowing a political appointee who was not a professional archivist or historian to make decisions about the historical records of the president and the country.

Later that same year, Congress passed the Presidential Recordings and Materials Preservation Act of 1974. It canceled Nixon's agreement with Sampson and established guidelines to control access to the materials. In 1987 the first of the 4,000 hours of tapes made in the Oval Office were released for listening at the National Archives, and more continue to be made available to the public. The Watergate tapes, as they are sometimes called, are invaluable not only for documenting a president's controversial actions but also for illuminating just how executive decisions were made in the years 1969–1974.

At Odds with GSA

The National Archives continued to be at odds with the administrators of GSA. One administrator threatened to solve the Archives's persistent problem of lack of storage space by disbursing many of the records stored in Washington, D.C., to field branches. Historians and other researchers vehemently protested that their research would become nearly impossible because it would be too expensive to move from one field branch to another to carry out their research. In 1982, another administrator, faced with budget cuts, forced the entire GSA to reduce its staff drastically, which proved particularly damaging to the National Archives: About 200 skilled staff positions were eliminated and not replaced. He then took direct operational control of programs in the regional offices away from the archivist.

The National Archives's troubles with GSA began to raise an alarm in high places, so much so that finally, in 1980, some congressmen introduced a bill to make the National Archives independent again. No action was taken, so similar bills were introduced in 1981 and 1983. With support from historians, genealogists, librarians, archivists, and other groups, Congress passed the National Archives and Records Administration Act of 1984 to separate the two bodies.

Researchers in the manuscript research room at the National Archives. One way the Office of the National Archives works with the public is by providing reference service on the collection.

FOUR

The Agency at Work

On April 1, 1985, the National Archives once again opened its doors as an independent agency. The writers of the National Archives Act of 1984 put to an end the possibility that some of the mistakes of the past would recur. They specified that the agency be headed by the archivist of the United States, who would be appointed by the president with the advice and consent of the Senate "without regard to political affiliations and solely on the basis of the professional qualifications required to perform the duties and responsibilities of the office." The archivist would be free to set the priorities that best serve researchers, federal agencies, and the general public.

The 1984 legislation gave back to GSA the elements of records management it had been created to fulfill: It promotes economy and efficiency in the use of forms, copying, office automation, and other areas. To the National Archives and Records Administration (NARA, the new name for NARS) it left the more fundamental job of ensuring that other federal agencies create records that tell the story of the organization, policies, and activities of the U.S. government. The Archives would of course also still ensure that records with permanent value are preserved and those with no future value are destroyed as scheduled.

Independence brought other changes to the National Archives, from reporting directly to Congress and the Office of Management and Budget (contacts formerly handled by GSA) to designing and printing stationery for each National Archives facility. Independence allowed the archivist to change the regional structure of the agency. When it was part of GSA, the National Archives had been divided into 10 regional offices, and, like GSA, each one had reported to GSA management. Archivist Robert M. Warner decided that his comparatively small agency would work most effectively without that supervisory regional structure. The field offices now report directly to the person in Washington who supervises their program.

Still, the National Archives is by no means small. Its 1,820 employees (as of September 30, 1987) are split roughly between the Washington area and the field branches. About 1,200 additional temporary employees staff the field branches, many of them working summers pulling files for researchers. To enable the Archives to reach and organize the widely disbursed array of American historical documents, the agency is divided into seven major offices, each one headed by an assistant archivist who is responsible for that program.

Three of the offices, those of Records Administration, Federal Records Centers, and the Federal Register, work primarily with other federal agencies. In contrast, another three, the Offices of the National Archives, Presidential Libraries, and Public Programs, chiefly serve researchers and the public. The seventh, the Office of Management and Administration, handles budget planning, personnel matters, and the like for all the other offices. Such special staffs as Congressional Relations, Legal Services, and Public Affairs report directly to the archivist or his deputy. (The work of two more of these staffs, the Archival Research and Evaluation staff and the Life Cycle Coordination staff, are described in chapter six.)

Deciding the Fate of the Files

The Office of Records Administration, created after the National Archives regained independence, handles most of NARA's records-management responsibilities. Staff members prepare publications to explain records management and offer training programs for personnel in other agencies. If an agency has a particular records-management problem, archivists in the Office of Records Administration will help the agency find a solution. The EPA recently called in the office's staff to advise it on training its own records-management team.

Some of the most challenging jobs in the National Archives are in this branch, for the skills require some ability to predict as well as a solid idea of what the entire government is engaged in doing. These archivists must decide the fate of all federal records—whether the information will be kept or destroyed. They must gauge whether the records show vital or nonvital activities, organization, and policies of that government agency or if the information they contain has significant value for researchers. If so, the records must be kept permanently in the National Archives. If not, they are destroyed. Part of the process is distinguishing the daily management of, for example, the Department of Housing and Urban Development from what embodies an important policy as it is put through—in other words, what is a by-product of government activity and what is the activity itself. Some records do not fit easily into one category, whereas others, in the eyes of an archivist, may be both. To complicate matters further, records come in many forms—papers, maps, photographs, motion pictures, microfilm, sound recordings, electronic files, and more—and all must be evaluated.

The decision to keep or destroy is made about series of records, not individual ones. For instance, an archivist would decide the fate of the pay records of the entire Social Security Administration, not the paper that documented the raise of one worker. Agencies submit lists of series of records and propose either their eventual destruction or their eventual transfer to the National Archives. Archivists review these lists and, for those to be destroyed, rule on the length of the retention period. Through years of this appraisal work, archivists have developed disposition schedules for series common to most agencies, and, as one might guess, only a small percentage are considered permanently valuable.

Most records now created by government agencies already have disposition schedules, but some older records, and even some more current ones, must be appraised. For instance, in 1987 archivists in the Office of Records Administration appraised National Oceanic and Atmospheric Administration (NOAA) records about the wreck of the U.S.S. *Monitor.* During the Civil War, the first battle between ironclad ships was fought in 1862 by the *Monitor* and the Confederate ship *Virginia.* The *Monitor* later sank. Its wreck was not found until 1973, and in 1975 the NOAA designated its site as the first National Marine Sanctuary. NOAA controls underwater access to the ship and has supervised scientific investigations, the recovery of artifacts, and studies of the unique ship. Archivists appraised NOAA records about the *Monitor,* and among the records they considered permanent is correspondence relating to the site and studies of artifacts, as well as underwater slides, motion pictures, and videotapes of the ship.

In another appraisal project, NARA accepted original printed posters and

When the sunken Civil War ironsides U.S.S. Monitor *was found off the coast of North Carolina in 1973, information and records on various artifacts, such as this lantern, were evaluated by the National Archives and added to its permanent files about the ship.*

related textual records from the Smokey the Bear program of the Forest Service. Dating from the 1940s to the early 1980s, these records trace the development of the Smokey the Bear and fire-prevention programs.

The Records Centers

Because office space is expensive, only records needed for daily use are kept in offices. When an agency no longer needs a group of records daily or needs them only occasionally, it retires the records to a storage area, often a federal records center.

Although most records are scheduled for eventual destruction, many must be retained temporarily to comply with legal, fiscal, or other requirements. The Office of Federal Records Centers offers agencies economical storage of

The Archives's collection of records from the Smokey the Bear campaign (dating from the 1940s to the 1980s) traces the development of the Forest Service's fire-prevention program.

the records they no longer use daily. Records centers are similar to large warehouses and are often located on the outskirts of metropolitan areas, where land and buildings are relatively inexpensive. NARA has 14 records centers throughout the country. Records do not stay in a center indefinitely, but are retained according to a schedule. At the end of their scheduled time they are either destroyed or brought permanently into the National Archives.

Nearly all federal agencies use the records centers, but the biggest users are the Treasury Department, especially its Internal Revenue Service, and the Department of Defense. The records centers provide reference service on the records in their custody. The most frequent requests are for IRS tax returns (for people or companies being audited) and Social Security claim folders.

Records centers also provide courtesy storage for the inactive papers of any member of Congress during the term in office. Because the papers of a member of Congress are considered personal papers, not federal records, they must be removed from the records center when the member leaves office—the National Archives does not have the authority to accept the papers of 535 members of Congress, as it does those of a president. Often a member of Congress donates his or her papers to the home state's historical society or to the state university's library, where researchers can more easily use them.

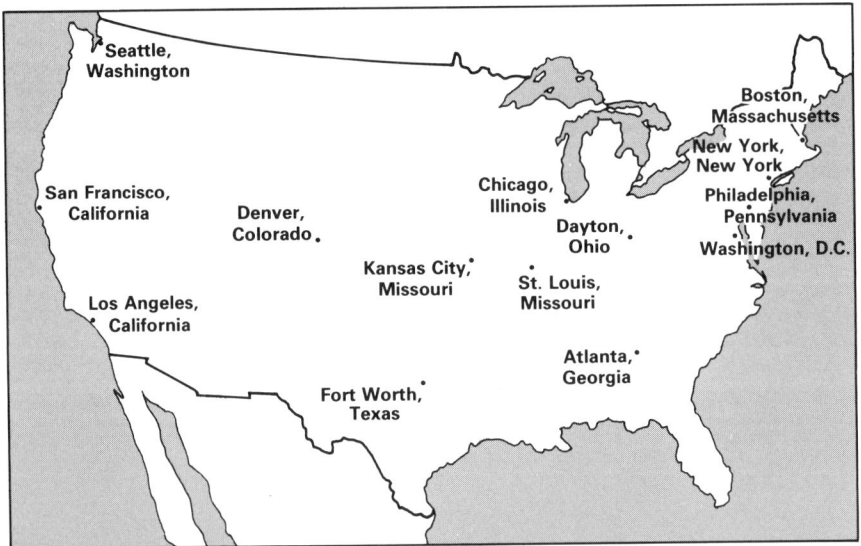

The National Archives has 14 records centers located across the country to provide reference service and storage space for valuable records, including papers, maps, photographs, and motion pictures.

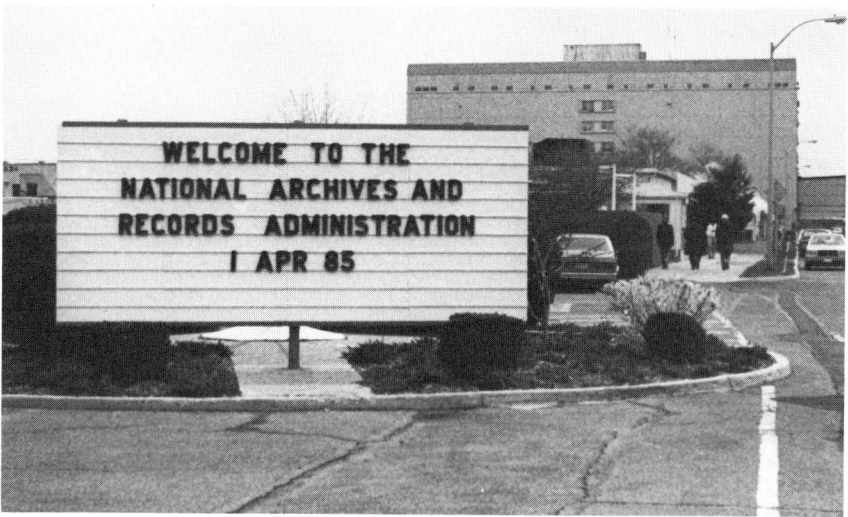

The records center and regional branch in Bayonne, New Jersey. Among the holdings of this center are the papers of the presidential committee appointed by President Richard M. Nixon and Luis Ferrer, governor of Puerto Rico, in 1970 to investigate the Puerto Ricans' right to vote for president and vice-president of the United States.

The records of former federal civilian and military personnel are housed in the two separate buildings of the National Personnel Records Center in St. Louis, Missouri. Each year the center answers nearly 2 million requests for information from these files. The requests often concern claims for benefits, such as retirement pay.

Office of the Federal Register

The third office within NARA that primarily serves federal agencies is the Office of the Federal Register (OFR). This office publishes the official text of laws, administrative regulations, and presidential documents for the government. For more than 50 years it has produced the daily *Federal Register,* which publishes presidential proclamations and executive orders and current and proposed regulations of federal agencies. It also publishes any document that must by statute be made public, covering the entire range of government activities from consumer product safety to environmental protection to occupational health and safety.

In 1937 the Archives began the first compilation of all government regulations. Called the *Code of Federal Regulations,* it was completed in 1947 when the last of 15 volumes was published. Each year the OFR updates the code by including the changes in regulations printed in the daily *Federal Register.* By the end of September 1987, the code had grown to 102,229 pages in 168 volumes.

The three branches of the federal government perform an ever-expanding amount of work, and all of it bears on the public. The Office of the Federal Register keeps on top of it in a number of forms. In the *Codification of Presidential Proclamations and Executive Orders,* this office provides another central source of information about proclamations and orders from the president. It also issues the *Weekly Compilation of Presidential Documents,* which prints the presidential speeches, transcripts of news conferences, messages, and other materials made public by the White House each week—everything from the suspension of diplomatic relations with a foreign power to holiday greetings for the nation. These are compiled annually into the *Public Papers of the President.*

Before 1950 every law passed in Congress was published by the Department of State; that responsibility was then given to the Office of the Federal Register. A few days after a law is passed, the OFR publishes a slip law (in other words, a pamphlet). At the end of each session of Congress, the laws and resolutions enacted that session are compiled and published as the *United States Statutes at Large.* This volume also includes proposed and ratified amendments to the Constitution and presidential proclamations. In recent years, the most heated debates in the first category have been over the proposed Equal Rights Amendment (the ERA, on women's rights), and whether the Constitution should be amended to require a balanced budget.

The OFR also publishes the annual *United States Government Manual.* A central source of information about the legislative, judicial, and executive agencies, it serves as the official handbook of the federal government by describing briefly the history, organization, and programs of each branch. It also includes information about quasi-official agencies, such as the Smithsonian Institution, and some international organizations, such as the United Nations, in which the United States participates. The manual has a name index of high-level agency officials and a list of commonly used abbreviations and acronyms in the government.

The information on government regulations published by the OFR affects all Americans and their businesses. The legal profession, government contractors, trade associations, consumer organizations, and other groups depend on

66

these publications for information about the government and what it proposes to do. Toward this end, the OFR gives workshops on how to use the sources effectively (often attended by librarians who then help others use the publications) and on how to draft legal documents (for executive-agency personnel who must write regulations clearly and concisely).

The OFR has several responsibilities other than publications. At election time, the president and vice-president are technically elected not by popular vote but by the electoral college, representatives chosen by popular vote from each state who formally cast their state's votes for president and vice-president. When each state's electors meet, they sign and seal six lists of their votes. Three copies of these certificates of election are sent to their state officials, and one copy to Congress. The other two copies are sent to the archivist of the United States, who passes them to the OFR; it keeps one copy free for public inspection and the other in reserve, available to Congress if something should happen to its copy.

The archivist has also delegated another important responsibility to this office. When Congress proposes an amendment to the Constitution, three-fourths of the states must ratify it before it becomes valid. The OFR circulates the official text of the amendment to the states. If a state ratifies the amendment, it sends back its certificate of ratification. The office keeps count of the ratifications, and when three-fourths of the states have ratified the amendment and it is thereby adopted, the archivist informs Congress.

Office of the National Archives

Whereas the three above-mentioned offices all serve the public (sometimes indirectly), they deal primarily with other government agencies. In contrast, the Office of the National Archives (ONA) works most often with the public. When researchers visit the National Archives, they usually work with staff from this office, whose name indicates its focal role in the whole of the National Archives. The ONA has custody of the records with historical importance or with enough research value to be permanently preserved. Its responsibilities include accessioning, preserving, and providing reference services on these records.

The ONA accessions records in their many formats—paper, videotape, maps, photographs, and others. For example, it has accessioned the records of the Commission on the Space Shuttle Challenger Accident. Most of those records are on paper and microfilm, but the collection also includes sound recordings of the commission's hearings and of the craft's brief flight and computer tapes that contain digital information on the flight.

After it accessions the records, the ONA is then responsible for preserving them and making them available for research. Reference service may be provided in many ways. It may mean physically handing records to a researcher in a research room at the National Archives or answering a letter requesting information from the records. Or it may mean preparing a microfilm publication that will reproduce those series of records most heavily used by researchers. In many instances, the ONA also provides researchers with copies of records.

Closely related to this reference work is the systematic review of security-classified records that are more than 30 years old to determine if they may be

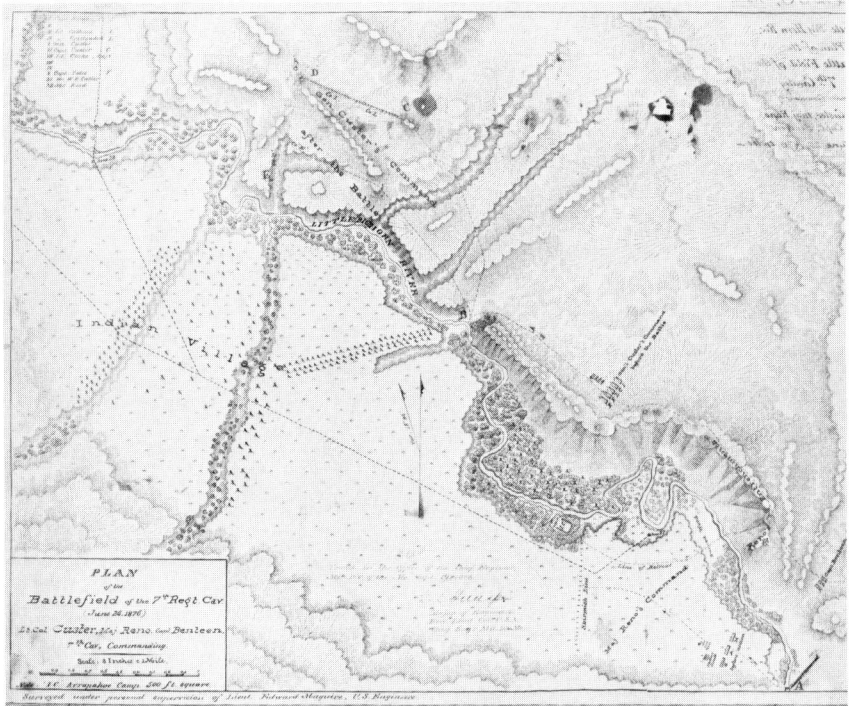

The National Archives has a large collection of historically significant maps, such as this one of the battlefield at Little Big Horn, where Sioux and Cheyenne Indians defeated Major General George A. Custer in 1876. Historians study battlefield maps to better understand military tactics.

The explosion of the space shuttle Challenger *on January 28, 1986. The Office of the National Archives accessions a variety of records, including this photograph from the records of the Commission on the Space Shuttle* Challenger *Accident.*

released to the public. To make such a delicate decision, the staff uses guidelines prepared by whichever federal agency originally classified the document or, if the original agency no longer exists, the agency that now has jurisdiction over the information. (Such a case is the CIA's handling of OSS secrets from World War II.) If a body of records has classified information scattered throughout, the staff must review the series page by page. From September 1986 to September 1987, the staff in the ONA and in Presidential Libraries reviewed 7,077,951 pages.

If in the course of his or her studies a researcher encounters a notice that a document has been withdrawn from a series because it contains classified information, he or she may formally request a *declassification review*. The National Archives then refers the document to the responsible agency and the agency reviews it for possible release.

A declassification hearing. Archivists with security clearance periodically review the records labeled as classified by their originating agency. A researcher may also request a declassification review of documents he or she wishes to see.

The Field Branches

The Office of the National Archives has field branches in Boston, New York, Philadelphia, Atlanta, Chicago, Kansas City, Fort Worth, Denver, Los Angeles, San Francisco, and Seattle. Each branch provides a full range of archival activities, from reference service to public programs, and each serves as a storehouse for records on local and regional history, which are usually accessioned from the regional offices of federal agencies.

Though most federal agencies have headquarters in Washington, D.C., many of them also have offices throughout the country. Sometimes the records created in these field offices are similar in content or scope to those at the headquarters, and sometimes they are not. The National Archives did a number of studies to determine how to best serve the researchers before setting up its own regional archives branches—would it be most convenient for all of an agency's records to be in Washington, or would researchers prefer to have matters of local interest remain in the region? The studies showed that the local records should remain close to their source, so beginning in 1969 the Archives launched its regional branches.

The two largest categories of records in the regional branches are about the law (from district courts) and about the land (from the Department of the

Interior). Each region also has many other types of records of local interest. The Fort Worth branch, for instance, keeps a large collection of records from the Bureau of Indian Affairs about the American Indians of the southwestern states. The Atlanta branch has a wealth of material on the Tennessee Valley Authority and its land-use and electrification projects. The Los Angeles and San Francisco branches have records about immigrants from Asia. In addition to records of local interest, each regional branch has on microfilm some of the most popular records in Washington, D.C. For example, a researcher may find in any field branch a microfilm copy of the Papers of the Continental Congress or the census schedules, the raw data collected during house-by-house surveys done by canvassers every 10 years.

The Tennessee Valley Authority (TVA) built the Loudon Dam on the Tennessee River in 1942. The National Archives's regional branch near Atlanta, Georgia, contains records on the TVA and its construction of dams and power plants.

The John F. Kennedy Library

The John F. Kennedy Library honors our youngest elected president by capturing the spirit of public service he exemplified. The library sits on Columbia Point beside Massachusetts Bay in a parklike environment of dune grass, pine trees, and wild roses, a few miles south of downtown Boston. The striking design is the work of renowned architect I. M. Pei.

A tour of the library's museum begins with a 30-minute film about Kennedy's life. One highlight is an excerpt from Kennedy's 1960 inaugural address, in which he delivered his famous line, "Ask not what your country can do for you; ask what you can do for your country." In the exhibit hall runs an illustrated timeline to help visitors recall the broader perspective of world and American history in the early 1960s. Among the displays, visitors can see Kennedy's favorite rocking chair (he suffered from back pain) and a coconut with the message Kennedy scratched onto it after the boat he commanded, the PT-109, was sunk in the Pacific by the Japanese during World War II. The museum also features displays on the Cuban Mis-

The John F. Kennedy Library, near Boston, Massachusetts, preserves Kennedy's presidential papers as well as film footage from his press conferences.

sile Crisis (1962), the Nuclear Test-Ban Treaty he signed with the Russians (1963), and the Peace Corps, which he helped launch. A favorite stop in the museum for many visitors is the theater that screens excerpts from Kennedy's press conferences. His wit and charm are brought alive in this footage, a reminder of his skillful use of the medium of television.

After touring the museum, some visitors may not realize that there is much more here than the exhibits. Like the other parts of the National Archives, the Kennedy library holds part of the documentary heritage of the United States, in this case the presidential papers from the Kennedy administration. These include White House files and papers donated by some of his cabinet officials and advisers. The site is also home to the papers from his years as a congressman and a senator, as well as his brother Bobby Kennedy's papers.

All of the National Archives's nine presidential libraries contain many photographs, motion pictures, and oral history interviews with people associated with the president, and the Kennedy library is no exception. One of the unexpected additional highlights here are some papers and manuscripts from the writer Ernest Hemingway. (The two men's widows arranged the donation.) Again like the other presidential libraries, the Kennedy library encourages wide use of its documentary holdings by historians and other scholars.

President Kennedy looks at a bust of Franklin D. Roosevelt during his visit to the FDR Library in 1960

The Kennedy library uses these vast resources to convey Kennedy's enthusiasm for the American system of politics and government and to demonstrate how he put his energy to work. The library staff reaches out to a broad community by holding seminars for local university professors so that they can suggest to their students how to use the library. The staff also works with high school teachers to develop programs for their students, who can then use the library's archival sources in American history and government classes.

The John F. Kennedy Library is dedicated to the 35th president of the United States. It is also dedicated to those who, like Kennedy, seek a better world through the art of politics.

The Presidents' Papers

The treasures of the Office of Presidential Libraries also allow for research outside of Washington. Since the Franklin D. Roosevelt Library opened to tourists in 1941 (and to researchers in 1946), libraries have been built for Presidents Hoover, Truman, Eisenhower, Kennedy, Johnson, Ford, and Carter. Each library is in the president's hometown or home state—the Harry S. Truman Library is in his hometown of Independence, Missouri; the Jimmy Carter Library is in Atlanta, Georgia, where he served as governor. In 1988 the papers of President Nixon were still being administered by the National Archives in Washington, D.C., until a site could be chosen and a building constructed for his library, probably in his native state of California. About 1.5 million persons visit the libraries each year.

The libraries preserve and make available for research the papers and other historical materials of the recent presidents. Among the materials in each library are the president's White House files, materials accumulated by the president before and after his presidency, and papers donated by individuals who worked for or with the president. The libraries also have audiovisual

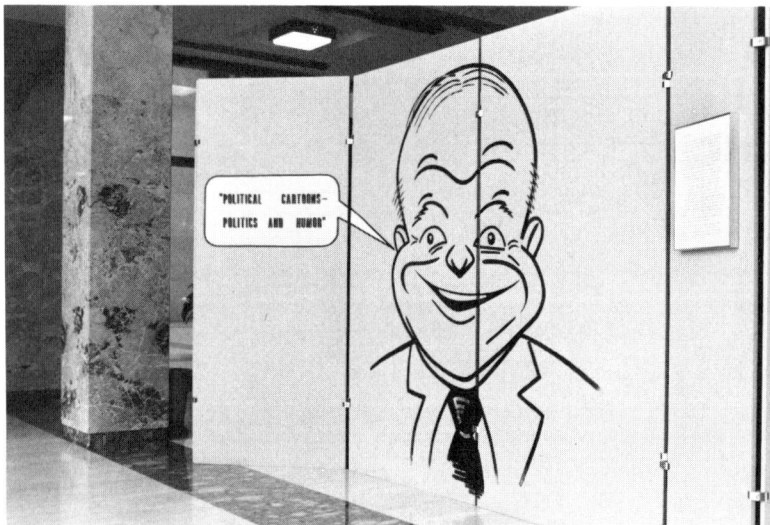

One cartoon in a exhibition at the Dwight D. Eisenhower Library in Abilene, Kansas. The National Archives's staff at presidential libraries preserves personal and official records of presidents and prepares historic documents and memorabilia for exhibits.

materials and oral histories, as well as three-dimensional objects that may be displayed in the museum that is part of each library. By opening their records to wide scholarly use and by preparing programs for the general public, the libraries aim to increase understanding of individual presidents as well as of the institution of the presidency and of the American political system.

When President Nixon signed an agreement with GSA Administrator Arthur F. Sampson after his resignation in 1974, he indirectly changed one aspect of how we can study the presidency. From George Washington's administration until that time, the papers of the president were considered his personal property, and each president could decide their fate. Even after presidential libraries were administered by NARA, Congress still considered the president's papers his own. But Congress objected to Nixon's agreement with Sampson (a political appointee) because it closed the papers to research for an exceptionally long time and allowed the destruction of some of the tape recordings Nixon had made. Whereas Congress had previously only encouraged the chief executive to donate his papers, now, for the first time, Congress *required* presidential materials to be deposited with the government. The Presidential Records Act of 1978 gave the government ownership of all presidential materials created after the term of office beginning January 20, 1981 (in other words, beginning with President Ronald Reagan's tenure). Thus ended the tradition of a president retaining private ownership of his papers.

In 1986 Congress grew concerned about the rising costs of the expanding presidential library system, for each one seemed to be bigger than the last. The Gerald R. Ford Library and Museum is in two separate buildings in two Michigan cities: the library in Ann Arbor, the museum in Grand Rapids—and Ford was president for only two and a half years. Of course, each time one president succeeds another, a new library and its costs are added to the system.

To keep the growing costs under control, Congress declared, in the Presidential Libraries Act of 1986, that each future presidential library be housed in only one building no larger than 70,000 square feet; 20 percent of the cost of the land and building must be covered by an endowment made up of private donations. Furthermore, the income from the endowment helps pay operating expenses. If a library is larger than 70,000 square feet, it must have additional endowment to pay for the costs of the extra space.

There is one more part of NARA aside from the six offices described here. The Office of Public Programs, along with the many special events and services provided by other offices, affords the average person the best glimpse into America's past through the National Archives.

A high school band plays at the Constitution Day celebration on the steps of the National Archives building. To promote interest in American history and its collections, the Archives organizes a variety of events for the public.

FIVE

Special Services and Programs

As it was first conceived, the National Archives would be a special service. What program could be less routine than the preservation of America's past? Yet the very scale of the undertaking demanded a large and rigorously arranged organization to keep the government's business properly on file. The largest part of work would be to keep on top of the situation, and the rest would be to inform the public of the vast amount of information within its reach and to exhibit what could safely be shown. Most of the special programs, services, and events the Archives now sponsors keep these goals uppermost.

The decades-long struggle to establish the agency gave historians and its other proponents time to prepare. Many advocates hoped that it could provide more than storage of historical records. They wanted the National Archives to serve the country, both the public and scholars, by building an appreciation of the value of historical records.

The Founding Fathers' Works

As one way to encourage the widespread availability and appreciation of historical documents, J. Franklin Jameson used his considerable influence to encourage the publication of historical documents by the government. In 1934 the NHPC was created to "make plans, estimates, and recommendations for such historical works and collections of sources as seem appropriate for publication . . . at the public expense." Although it was to be a separate organization, the archivist would chair the NHPC, and the Archives would provide support for it.

The NHPC first met on January 29, 1935. Among its earliest activities was its recommendation to Congress, in 1936, that a publication be issued to help celebrate the sesquicentennial (150th anniversary) of the Constitution. Congress reserved for itself the right to approve each project recommended by the commission and make appropriation for it, but it did not act on this or later recommendations. After World War II and the pressure of war work at the Archives had let up, the commission became active again in the 1950s. Archivist Wayne C. Grover fought to keep the NHPC part of the Archives when the rest of his agency was part of GSA, and he hoped to renew the commission's work as a way to increase the Archives's visibility in the historical community.

When the first volume of *The Papers of Thomas Jefferson* was published, in 1950, those interested in a renewed NHPC presented a copy to President Harry S. Truman. Known for his interest in history, Truman was intrigued by the volume and urged the publication of more writings by important figures in American history. Truman asked the commission to poll some historians and then recommend what to publish.

A signal event in the growth of the National Archives came when Truman signed the Federal Records Act of 1950. Among other things, it strengthened the NHPC by enlarging the membership of the commission, allowing it to hire a staff, and charging it with cooperating with states, localities, and private groups in editing and publishing important historical papers. Perhaps most important, the act eliminated the impractical requirement that Congress approve each project.

These changes gave the NHPC new life, and since 1951 it has thrown its support behind more than 250 documentary publication projects. In 1964 new legislation further expanded its powers by giving it money to grant directly to the programs it supports. (Previously, the commission could only endorse projects and help them locate private money.) In 1975 the commission's program was expanded yet again to include a records program and so became the National Historical Publications and Records Commission (NHPRC). The records program allows the commission to give grants to state and local governments, historical societies, archives, libraries, and associations to preserve, arrange, and describe historical records. The grants have helped pay for both printed and microfilmed records. The National Archives has had a training program for archivists since 1938, but these new grants also gave the NHPRC the means to support training and development programs outside of NARA.

Some eminent Americans have been served by the publications program: Diplomats, politicians, reformers, scientists, labor figures, and others have become better known thanks to the dispatch of their papers. The papers of George Washington, Martin Luther King, Jr., Jane Addams, and Benjamin Franklin are a few of those published with aid from the commission. Some corporations and organizations have also benefited from the publication of their records, such as the *Papers of the Society of American Indians for 1909–24*. The NHPRC has also supported the publication of the *Documentary History of the Ratification of the Constitution* and the *Documentary History of the Supreme Court of the United States, 1789–1800.*

The records program, in a similar manner, supports efforts to preserve and make available such items as state, county, or municipal government records as well as manuscripts, personal papers, and family or corporate archives. Special collections in particular fields of study, including the arts, business, education, ethnic and minority groups, immigration, labor, and politics have also been gathered and preserved. For example, Boston had never had a municipal archives program. Some of the city's records had been saved by local organizations, including Harvard University, the Boston Public Library, and the Massachusetts Historical Society, but many had been lost or destroyed. Then, in 1985, the NHPRC gave the city of Boston a grant to draw up plans for a municipal archives and records-management program. The money was to be used to create the position of city archivist, survey the records, outline further action, and publish a report of findings and recommendations. The result is a plan to preserve Boston's past. Another 1985 grant gave money to the University of Missouri to preserve the collection of photographs from its annual news-photograph contest.

The Audiovisual Center

NARA also directs the National Audiovisual Center, which helps the public use audiovisual programs produced by the government. The center, established in 1969, is self-supporting within the National Archives. It serves as central information point, depository, and sales outlet for all the government agencies' audiovisual programs, making them available to government and the public. In a variety of formats, more than 2,800 titles may be bought or rented. They cover a wide range of topics, including drug education, national parks, and the armed forces. The National Audiovisual Center also collects data on purchases, production, and duplication of audiovisual programs by federal agencies. These data are used by Congress and the Office of Management and Budget and are available to government agencies and the public.

Fighting Time and the Elements

Throughout every program in the National Archives runs a common concern: the preservation of the records under its domain. Paper records are fragile and deteriorate very quickly if not given proper care; a newspaper left to the elements over just a few hours, for example, will turn yellow. Archivists must care for millions of pages of paper. Other types of records, such as photographs or magnetic tape, may be equally fragile. Archivists must ensure that they, too, are preserved permanently. How do they do it?

This decomposed nitrate film reel demonstrates how vulnerable records are to the elements. Archivists try to prevent the deterioration of film by providing a controlled environment.

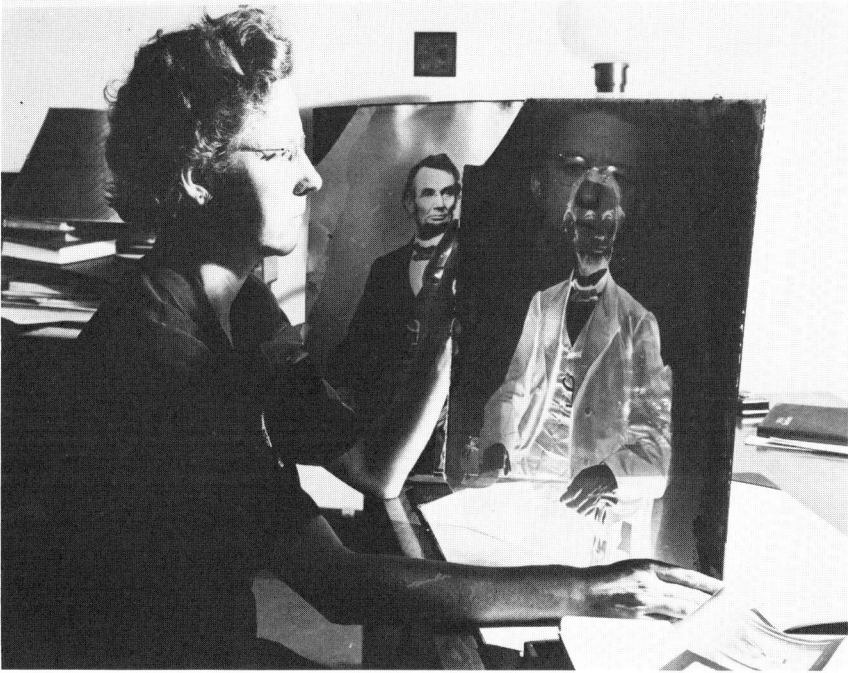

Mathew Brady's glass-plate negatives of the Civil War, including this portrait of Abraham Lincoln, are carefully preserved in an atmosphere-controlled room at the National Archives.

First, archivists try to provide the right environment for each type of record, one that will forestall its deterioration. The preservation staff in the Office of the National Archives has been working through the National Information Standards Organization to have a standard for storage of paper adopted by the American National Standards Institute. The standard will suggest the best temperature and relative humidity for paper and will specify limits for substance particles and pollutant gases in the air. Rapid fluctuations or extremes of temperature and relative humidity, as well as pollution in the air, speed the deterioration of paper. These standards will guide the National Archives in providing the best environment for the preservation of paper within its buildings.

Other media besides paper require their own special environments. For example, the National Archives has photographs and negatives of the Civil War made by the leading photographer of the day, Mathew Brady, and similar materials on the exploration of the American West from the latter half of the

19th century. These negatives need delicate handling and, unlike modern negatives on film, are on glass. A custom-designed, room-sized vault is being built within the National Archives building to store these valuable photographic records. The room, which is to be completed by 1990, will have a separate air-conditioning, purification, and filtering system; the fire protection system will not use water but a gas, halon, that smothers flames. All cabinets and materials in the room will be analyzed and tested to ensure that they will not damage the fragile materials in the room.

Another step in preservation care is called *holdings maintenance.* Archivists try to prevent damage and to slow the inevitable deterioration that comes with age by properly housing the records. Because storing papers in acidic folders or boxes hastens their deterioration, archivists use special acid-free containers. Simple steps such as removing staples or flattening folded papers also prolong a document's life. Thin, weak paper or pages that are handled often are placed in protective polyester sleeves, as are maps and other large items.

Some records used very often by researchers need still more protection. Census records, for example, are used hundreds of times each day by genealogists and others. Such records may be reproduced on other media,

An archivist examines documents that have been laminated (sealed in plastic) by the Document Restoration Branch.

perhaps photocopies or, more often, microfilm. Researchers use these copies so that the valuable originals are rarely handled and unlikely to be damaged. An additional advantage of microfilmed records is that they may be copied and distributed for use or sale in all the field branches.

Caring for the Charters

The most public preservation challenge for the National Archives is its care, since 1952, of the Declaration of Independence, the Constitution, and the Bill of Rights. Known as the *Charters of Freedom,* these three documents are permanently displayed in the rotunda of the Archives's exhibition hall.

Visitors immediately notice how difficult it is to read the Declaration of Independence. It is more than 200 years old, but the document long ago began to show its age, because through the years its display under harmful conditions—and attempts to reproduce it—have damaged the parchment and faded the ink.

To shield it, the Archives keeps each parchment page in a separate sealed case of protective glass and bronze. Each case contains only the inert gas helium and a carefully measured amount of water vapor. Elements that might damage the documents, such as dust, mold, too much or too little moisture, and sulphur and other pollutants, are kept out of the cases. The documents are never removed from these cases, eliminating any chance of damage from improper handling or abrasion. Because the ultraviolet radiation in light, especially sunlight, can harm the documents, the light level in the exhibition hall is kept low and is carefully monitored. Special glass panels in the display cases have green filters to prevent ultraviolet and other harmful light from reaching the documents.

The Archives wants to keep the fundamental charters on display for all to see, but equally important, it must protect the documents from any further harm. When the exhibition hall is open and they are on display, a guard is always stationed next to them. If the guard should sense that the Charters are in danger, he or she can lower them in about one minute into a vault 20 feet below the floor of the exhibition hall by pressing a button. In case of power failure, a backup mechanism can also lower the documents and close the vault, which is constructed of steel and reinforced concrete with floor, walls, and lid each about 15 inches thick. The Charters are stored in this vault when not on display.

In the 1980s the National Archives introduced a new technology into its care

The Travels of the Declaration of Independence

Every July 4, Americans come together for picnics and fireworks to celebrate Independence Day, for on that date in 1776, the Continental Congress adopted the Declaration of Independence. On August 2, a beautifully written copy on parchment was ready, and the delegates to the Congress began to sign. But when visitors see the Declaration of Independence today at the National Archives, they immediately notice that it is worn and the signatures are barely legible. How did the document we so honor become so damaged?

After the statement cutting our ties with Britain was adopted, the Continental Congress ordered that several copies be printed and distributed around the country. Many of these broadsides, made by Philadelphia printer John Dunlap, still exist, including one in the National Archives. Later, the Declaration was *engrossed* on a large sheet of parchment. (Engrossing is the process of writing an official document in large, clear handwriting.) John Hancock signed first, and eventually all 56 delegates signed.

The signed Declaration of Independence probably traveled with the Continental Congress as it moved from city to city during the revolutionary war. At that time, parchment was rolled from the top down for storage. Consequently, the signatures on the bottom of any page were often exposed and, because parchment does not absorb ink, abrasion soon made the ink flake off, especially from the signatures.

When the federal government was formed in 1776, its seat moved from New York to Philadelphia and then to Washington, D.C. Because of the war, the Continental Congress met in 10 cities between 1776 and 1789, and the Declaration probably traveled with it to each city. Yet even when the government was settled, the Declaration still had three more trips to come.

The first came when the city of Washington was threatened by invading British soldiers during the War of 1812. A clerk in the State Department, which had custody of the document, packed it with other important records. Eventually they were taken to safety in Leesburg, Virginia, where they were being kept when the British burned Washington in August 1814. The Declaration was returned to the city the next month once the British troops had withdrawn.

Ironically, it was over the next 62 years of staying in the capital that the document suffered some of the worst damage. In 1826, to celebrate the Declaration's 50th anniversary, Secretary of State John Quincy Adams commissioned a facsimile of the fading document. Unfortunately, the technique used, called a *wet sheet transfer,* probably removed some of the ink. The document was laid over a copper plate, etched onto it, and printed. The result was good quality facsimiles, but some of the ink was left on the copper plate.

Until 1876 the Declaration was on display in the Patent Office along with George Washington's commis-

In 1953 the Declaration of Independence and the Constitution were transported via tank and with an armed escort from the Library of Congress to the National Archives.

sion as commander in chief of the Continental army. The two documents, framed and hung on a wall across from a window, suffered exposure from the damaging effects of sunlight.

The Declaration again briefly left Washington in 1876, when Philadelphia hosted the Centennial National Exposition. Millions of people viewed it, and the damage was becoming apparent. When it returned to Washington, its site in the State Department library left it exposed to fireplace smoke. Finally, in 1894, the State Department, concerned by the rapid fading and the deterioration of the parchment, removed the Declaration from display and stored it in a steel case.

In 1921, the Declaration of Independence was transferred from the State Department to the Library of Congress. The new display case was a great improvement: double panes of plate glass that sandwiched a special gelatin film designed to limit the damage from light.

The Declaration stayed in this shrine from 1924 to 1941. Then, during World War II, Librarian of Congress Archibald MacLeish sent it to the safety of Fort Knox, Kentucky. It returned in the fall of 1944, when the danger of military attack had passed.

Scientific advances in the preservation of paper have since served the Declaration well. In 1951, the document was sealed in a thermopane glass case filled with helium gas and a carefully measured amount of humidity. The cases were equipped to screen out damaging light. Those same cases still do the job today.

Finally, in 1953, along with the Constitution, the Declaration of Independence was packed and transported—in a tank with an armed escort—to the National Archives building. There the two prized documents joined a third, the Bill of Rights (the first 10 amendments to the Constitution), for permanent display in the large rotunda designed for them. The environment is carefully controlled and the light level monitored to ensure that the elements do no further harm to the charters of freedom.

85

of the Charters. It contracted the Jet Propulsion Laboratory (JPL), in Pasadena, California, a division of the National Aeronautics and Space Administration, to design and build an electronic camera to monitor the documents' condition. This *electronic imaging system,* based on JPL's space research, takes precise pictures of the documents while they remain sealed in their cases. The camera is capable of making an image of very high resolution, each square inch being divided into 1,000 units called pixels and each pixel recording a thousand variations in the amount of reflected light. The pixels are then interpreted in digital code and analyzed by computer. By comparing pictures taken periodically in this way, the computer will detect even the subtlest change in a document.

Electronic imaging can be used by conservators to analyze documents other

Kenneth Harris, director of preservation policy and services, checks the Constitution's condition in the floor vault that drops each night, and in case of emergency, 20 feet below the Archives's main exhibition hall.

A conservator demonstrates the electronic imaging system used to monitor the condition of the Charters of Freedom. The system is also used to authenticate documents by analyzing them with the help of computer-coded photographs.

than the Charters. Once a valuable original has been photographed by the system, the photographs can be used for authentication, should that be necessary. The precise imaging creates a unique "fingerprint" of a document.

Some Recent Highlights

Nearly a million visitors each year see the Charters and other exhibits from the Archives's holdings, and they are often surprised by what is on view in the rotunda. In recent years, exhibits have included President Nixon's letter of resignation, the Louisiana Purchase Treaty of 1803, the oath of allegiance to the United States signed by the revolutionary war traitor Benedict Arnold, and even a recipe for scones sent by Queen Elizabeth II of England to President Eisenhower. An exhibition of posters, Uncle Sam Speaks, documented 200 years of communications from the government to the people in colorful and descriptive broadsides, placards, and signs. And an exhibit of photographs called The American Image included a portrait of Civil War general William

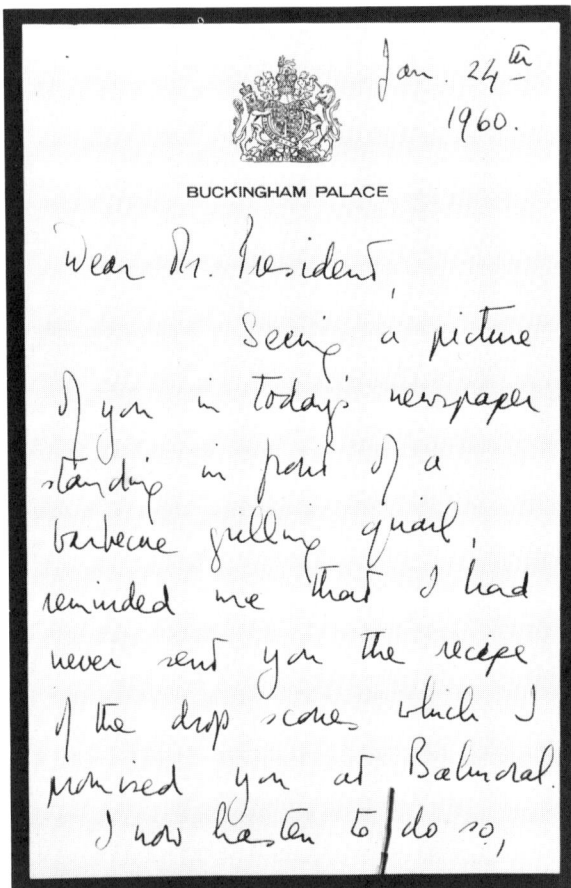

In 1960, Queen Elizabeth II of England sent a recipe for scones to President Dwight D. Eisenhower. Today the letter is in the National Archives.

Tecumseh Sherman wearing an armband of mourning after President Lincoln's assassination and Lewis Hine's photographs of child factory laborers in the early 20th century.

A 1988 exhibit, Living with the Constitution, which celebrated the bicentennial of the Constitution, included films of the 1963 contest of wills between Attorney General Robert F. Kennedy and Alabama governor George C. Wallace over the issue of desegregation. Kennedy had to send the National Guard to the University of Alabama, where Wallace was defying a court order that allowed black students to enroll in the all-white school. Also on display was a tape of President Lyndon Johnson introducing the 1965 Voting Rights Act.

(The act suspended the application of literacy tests used to discriminate against minorites in voting.)

Each of the presidential libraries has a museum for exhibits on the life and times of the presidents. Some include a reproduction of the Oval Office as it looked while that president was in office. The museums also develop new shows and display traveling exhibitions from other institutions. In one such show, in 1985, the Lyndon B. Johnson Library collaborated with the National Portrait Gallery to mount a major exhibition on Ulysses S. Grant in observance of the centennial of his death. In honor of the 150th anniversary of the founding of the Republic of Texas in 1836, the Johnson Library opened an exhibition about the four presidents who were instrumental in bringing Texas into the Union.

The National Archives field branches also hold exhibitions of archival material. The displays range in subject from the WPA to Buffalo Bill, the 19th-century scout and Wild West showman. The field branches loan exhibits for display at other local institutions as well.

Photographer Lewis Hine captured the grotesque exploitation of child laborers in the early 20th century. Many of Hine's photographs are in the National Archives.

The Harry S. Truman Library in Independence, Missouri, contains a replica of the Oval Office as it looked when Truman was president, from 1945 to 1953.

Programs for the Public

By far the most popular tourist attraction within the National Archives is the rotunda and exhibition hall in the National Archives building in Washington, D.C. The exhibitions in these areas are created by the Office of Public Programs (OPP), an office within NARA whose efforts are primarily directed to those outside of the agency.

The OPP works to encourage the general public to see and understand NARA's work and its holdings. In addition to its exhibition program, the OPP holds workshops every year on how to use the records and conducts special workshops to train teachers to use primary sources in the classroom. A large volunteer organization conducts tours of the building in Washington, D.C., and offers special tours and workshops for school groups. A tour may take a visitor through an exhibition or offer a behind-the-scenes look at the archivists' work.

The 1934 legislation that established the National Archives gave it authority to collect motion pictures. This collection, plus films made or acquired by other federal agencies and since accessioned by the Archives, serves as the basis of the film series the OPP offers. A 1988 film series, *Hollywood at War,* featured films made in prewar Hollywood that openly attacked Nazi ideology and were banned in many countries sympathetic to Germany.

Each year the National Archives holds two major public ceremonies to honor the Charters of Freedom. To celebrate the Declaration of Independence on July 4, an actor in colonial dress reads the Declaration on the grand stairs of the Constitution Avenue entrance to the rotunda. The event includes patriotic music and usually concludes with a demonstration, right on the street, of revolutionary war military tactics. The second such ceremony is on Constitution Day, September 17, when all four pages of the Constitution are displayed (usually, only the first and last pages are shown.) The celebration often includes a naturalization ceremony in which new citizens take the oath of allegiance while standing in front of the Constitution in its case.

The National Archives continues to search for new ways to let people know about the records it holds. In recent years, the OPP has introduced innovative programs to reach out to people. In one such program, the office jointly sponsored writing workshops with local playwrights who used archival records for creative material. During the celebration of the bicentennial of the

A guide (right) discusses a photograph with a visitor during a tour of an exhibition at the National Archives.

The National Archives's collection of film documentaries, from which this World War II still is taken, preserves actual footage of the war.

Constitution in September 1987, the dramatists staged two plays based on constitutional issues. The same celebration featured a play commissioned by the National Archives, *A Gallant and Lawless Act,* based on the writing of the Constitution.

Not all of the materials in the National Archives are created by the government. Some of them come from the public, and the OPP has acknowledged this fact. When the Gerald R. Ford Museum opened in 1981, an exhibit featured some of the handmade bicentennial gifts sent to President Ford in 1976. Another tribute to the public's interest in the government took a more dramatic turn: In August 1986 a group of actors hired by the OPP staged a short play called *Dear Uncle Sam,* based on some of the thousands of letters written to the government that are now found in the National Archives.

The OPP also organizes lunchtime lectures, often given by archivists on NARA's staff or researchers using NARA records, to offer the public an opportunity to learn more about records in the Archives. In January 1988, for example, Maurine H. Beasley, professor of journalism at the University of Maryland, discussed her book *Eleanor Roosevelt and the Media: A Public Quest for Self-Fulfillment,* researched at the Roosevelt Library, the National Archives, and elsewhere.

Some Helpful Publications

In a further effort to help the public use and understand its holdings, the OPP publishes books, guides, exhibit catalogs, leaflets, and a periodical. These publications offer assistance and information to a diverse audience. For instance, *A Guide to Civil War Maps in the National Archives* and *Guide to Genealogical Research in the National Archives* help researchers interested in specific subjects. Of more general interest are publications such as the series *Milestone Documents in the National Archives,* which reproduces some of the great documents that have shaped the course of U.S. history. Along with a reproduction of the featured document, each booklet contains a transcription for easier reading and an introduction that places the document in historical context. "Washington's Inaugural Address of 1789" and "The Emancipation Proclamation," to name two, are available in this series.

The OPP's quarterly journal, *Prologue,* brings to the public's attention the resources and programs of the National Archives, the regional archives, and the presidential libraries. Articles published in *Prologue* range from the general to the scholarly, and are usually based, in whole or in part, on the agency's holdings and programs.

The National Archives Trust Fund Board finances these publications, and it supports museum shops where visitors to the exhibition hall in Washington, D.C., and the presidential libraries purchase books, facsimile reproductions of

The research rooms at the National Archives and at the field branches are open to anyone wishing to use their primary source materials.

A National Archives–sponsored play, A Gallant and Lawless Act, *seen here being performed by the Paradise Island Express, entertained and educated Washington audiences during the summer of 1987. The play celebrated the Constitution's 200th birthday.*

historic documents, and souvenirs. These and all the other activities of the Office of Public Programs share the goal of letting people know what resources are available to them through the National Archives.

Doing Research at the Archives

Once a student of any age knows the tremendous range of the National Archives's holdings, getting one's hands on the material for research is the next step. This can be tricky, but the staff is equipped to field all questions.

Generally, research projects should not begin at the National Archives. Instead, researchers come there once they have done a great deal of work elsewhere, because the records at the National Archives are *primary sources*— the original speech, the unedited letters, the signed document, and so forth. *Secondary sources* are books, magazines, and articles that historians and others have written based on their knowledge of and research into a subject. (Abraham Lincoln's Gettysburg Address and other writings from his hand are primary sources; Stephen B. Oates's biography of Lincoln, which draws on a multitude of primary papers found at the Archives and elsewhere, is a secondary source on Lincoln and can be found in thousands of libraries.) Secondary sources often condense information available in primary sources and draw conclusions from this information. In order to use the primary sources effectively, one must first have used secondary sources extensively. Because

94

the National Archives has records of the federal government, the researcher should know which organizations within the government have dealt with his or her subject and when.

Guides to Research

The National Archives prepares and publishes several types of guides to help researchers use the records. The first source for researchers is the *Guide to the National Archives of the United States,* which gives a short description of all the record groups in the National Archives. Archivists prepare other types of guides, or *finding aids,* as they are called by archivists. The most common type of finding aid is a preliminary inventory. In these, researchers usually find an administrative history of the agency that created the records, brief descriptions of the type of records in each series, and perhaps a general description of the type of information available in the records.

A more unusual type of guide, but very useful when available, is a subject-matter guide that has been prepared by a staff member. In this type of guide, researchers learn which is the best series of records for information about a given subject, such as black history or World War I. There are other types of guides available, but the best guide for a beginning researcher is an experienced archivist.

Most researchers begin their work at the National Archives by discussing their research project with a reference archivist. He or she knows the records very well, how they are organized, and the most potentially fruitful places to look. A good archivist also knows the best sources in other branches and records groups.

In bringing the records to life for a wide audience, even for those who may never do research themselves, these many programs contribute to Washington's intellectual life and to a greater appreciation of our past throughout the country. The National Archives's special programs show that the records are preserved not just for historians and other scholars, but for everyone.

The agency's mission for the future grows more complicated as the government tackles a more complicated national and world situation. Funding shortages, political meddling, shortage of space, security constraints, and the most potentially harmful element of all, time itself, may conspire to keep some documents from those who own them—the American public. The last chapter will discuss some of these issues and how the National Archives fits into a larger world.

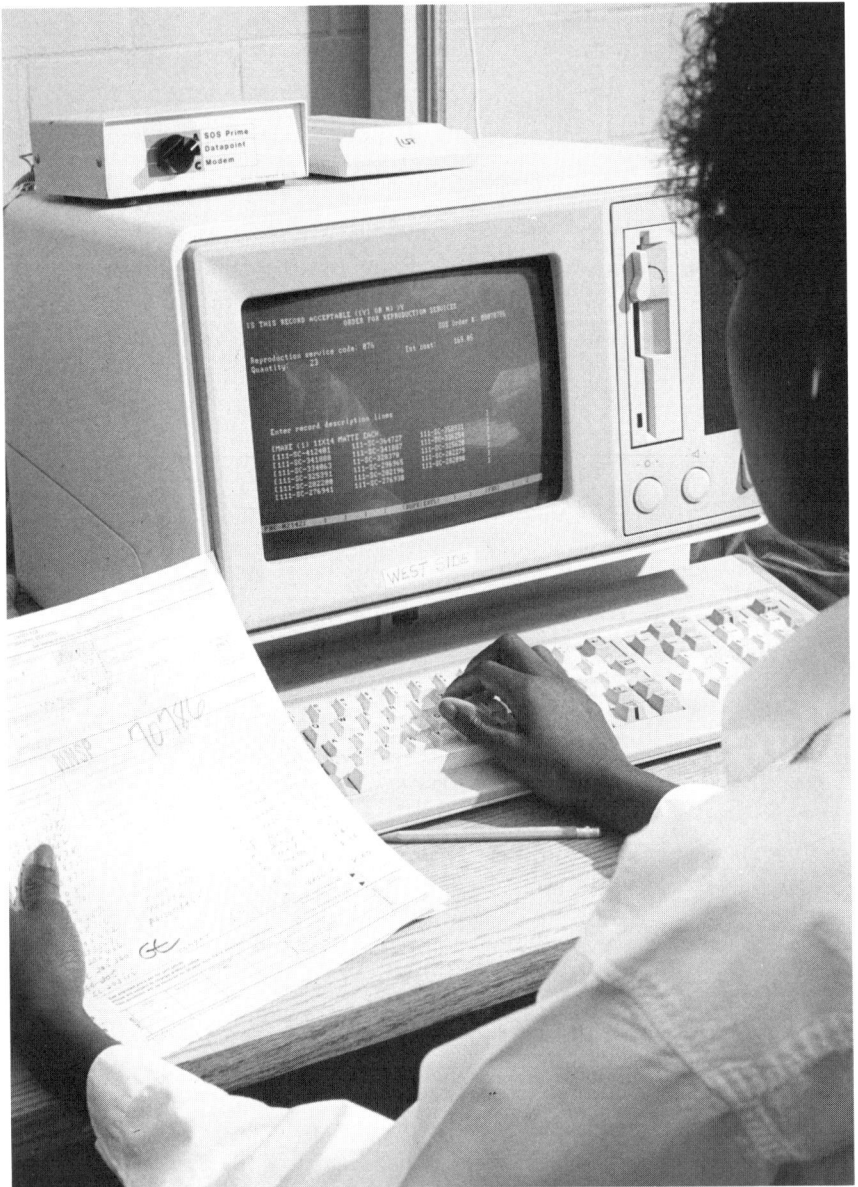

A National Archives employee uses a computer. Not only must the Archives utilize automation to handle its own records, but it must also manage the electronic records created by other agencies. Archivists face the challenge of preserving these particularly fragile records.

SIX

Future Challenges at the National Archives

Y ou don't have to go to Washington, D.C., to visit the National Archives," says the slogan at each of the field branches. In the National Archives's 1986 annual report, Acting Archivist of the United States, Frank G. Burke, noted with pride a significant fact: The National Archives has become a truly national agency. Across the country, 14 federal records centers, 11 federal branches, and 8 presidential libraries provide a nationwide network.

As proof of the public's growing awareness of this national network, in 1986, for the first time, more researchers paid visits to the field branches and presidential libraries than to the Washington-area facilities. In addition, the governors of the 50 states have each appointed a historical-records coordinator for their state to work with the NHPRC.

Historians and genealogists, the traditional users of the Archives, are now joined by the many others who have learned that primary sources are not just for scholars. People from all walks of life are attracted to the exhibits, lectures, workshops, film series, and tours given at both the central office and in the field branches. Symposia and conferences bring together people from such diverse fields as business, academia, and politics to make use of public records. The

Standing in front of a poster announcing an exhibition on the Crow Indians, a Seattle branch employee endorses the slogan on his button: You Don't Have to Go to Washington, D.C., to Visit the National Archives.

valuable historical film footage preserved by the National Archives is a boon to film and television producers. This part of the Archives is keeping up with the times, too: In 1986, more than 1,800 editions of "The MacNeil/Lehrer Newshour," a nightly Public Broadcasting System show often cited for the excellence of its coverage and presentation, were added to the film stacks. For as a clue to our society's character, the study of what happened yesterday is embellished by the study of how that news is presented in the media.

Putting Technology to Work

Staying abreast of changes is one of the National Archives's many challenges, in automation as well as in information itself. Introducing automation into its daily work makes the agency run more smoothly, from word processors that allow archivists to answer reference mail quickly and easily to budget and financial spread sheets and electronic mail systems that help the Archives run more efficiently. In using new computerized processes, the National Archives varies little from any other large, modern organization.

The Archives is a special case, of course, because of the volume it handles and because it must use automation to control its own records at the same time it handles the computer records created by other agencies. Adding to the challenge of managing electronic records is the rapid advance in technology that leads to constant change. Computers have used punch cards, magnetic tape, and disks to store information. Yet electronic records are particularly difficult to store because they are fragile and easy to erase. Perhaps more dangerous, their data are easy to alter.

Archivists must preserve the permanently valuable information stored by these different technologies. They must then decide whether it is best to preserve the information as it was created or whether it should be converted to another medium. In deciding, they must consider which medium will last the longest as well as which machines will still be available to read the information stored in that way. Experience with paper records tells an archivist that paper punch cards will last a long time; but in 50 years, will a machine exist to read punch cards?

With these taxing matters in mind, the Archivist created the Life Cycle Coordination Staff at NARA to develop new information systems that will track records through their entire life cycle. Records in any format will enter the NARA system while still in the creating agency when archivists first appraise and schedule them. They will be tracked until they are destroyed or accessioned by the National Archives. Then information about accessioned records may be added to a descriptive data base covering other records already in the National Archives. Another system will provide automated access to the holdings of the presidential libraries. The advantage is that for the first time, researchers will be able to find out from coordinated systems what records might interest them in any part of the National Archives's national network.

The archivist has appointed another group, the Archival Research and Evaluation Staff, to study new technologies and to assist other offices in applying them to their work. One of the most interesting uses of automation being explored by this staff is an attempt to develop an automated system that will mimic the human knowledge, judgment, and decision making of an experienced professional archivist. Currently, a knowledgeable archivist helps a researcher pinpoint the most useful records he or she needs. The new system would duplicate an archivist's judgment and knowledge with multifaceted indexing. This new "expert system," if successful, could be used as an aid to reference work or as a training tool for new archivists.

The Archives cannot delay in making its systems as effective as the new technology allows because the number of records increases every year.

In 1987, Don W. Wilson, former director of the Gerald R. Ford Library, was named the seventh archivist of the United States. His appointment assured that a qualified historian and archivist would be in charge well into the 1990s.

Old-fashioned paper records are bulky and therefore expensive to store. The National Archives building reached its record-storage capacity in the late 1960s, according to Dr. Don W. Wilson, who was sworn in as seventh archivist of the United States in December 1987. Computer records can be stored more efficiently, but most records accessioned by the Archives are not electronic.

Finding suitable storage space for the growing number of permanently valuable records is a constant challenge, and in 1988 Congress appropriated funds for the construction of a new archival facility—informally called "Archives II"—to enable the Archives to leave the 10 facilities it is leasing in the Washington area and to consolidate its operations. The building, which is to be constructed on the campus of the University of Maryland in College Park beginning in 1990, will include 1.7 million square feet for records storage and program support areas, space for approximately 775 employees and a minimum of 50,000 researchers a year, and additional space for the construction of new wings to accommodate future storage needs. The new building will not replace the Archives building in Washington—both will operate as archival facilities, but they will focus on different programs: The Archives building will continue to emphasize record storage and public activities; Archives II will provide state-of-the-art archival storage, laboratories, offices, a theater, and reference and conference rooms.

100

Part of a Larger World

As a leader in the international field of archival practices and theory, the National Archives of the United States serves the world as well as American citizens. The recent improvement in political relations between the United States and communist nations has benefited all: In 1987, working through the American Council of Learned Societies (a national professional organization that promotes the humanities and social sciences), Acting Archivist Frank G. Burke helped to arrange an exchange of archival staff and publications with the Soviet Union. The year before, Burke visited the People's Republic of China for the 60th anniversary celebration of that nation's archives.

Cooperation extends from the formal to the substantial. West Germany mounted a large exhibit on Baron Friedrich Wilhelm von Steuben, the German-born general of American forces in the revolutionary war who later became an American citizen, borrowing much of the material on his later life from the National Archives. In 1983, at the request of the Swedish embassy, the Archives arranged a brief display in the Capitol of the first treaty between Sweden and the United States. (Sweden was the first foreign state to recognize the new American republic, in 1783.) Other items in Washington, D.C., testify to America's place in world history, including the deed of gift for the Statue of Liberty given by the government and people of France in 1886 and a copy of the original charter of the United Nations from 1946. In a more ominous vein, the ongoing search for Nazi war criminals has often led to military records held at the National Archives—former UN secretary general Kurt Waldheim's activities as a Nazi officer in Yugoslavia were first revealed in 1985 in papers at the Archives. Looking more to the future, members of the conservation staff of NARA have hosted archivists from Central and South America to share ideas about how best to keep their nations' documents in usable shape. Indeed, virtually every state, local, university, and corporate archives in the country and around the world looks to the National Archives to take the lead in spirit and in fact as it solves new problems in archival science.

A Free and Open Society

The preservation of a nation's documents serves far more than a few people's interest in history. It is no coincidence that the idea of a formal national archives arose around the same time as the world's first free republics were

The 1876 deed of gift of the Statue of Liberty is kept in a vault at the National Archives. The statue, dedicated 10 years later, was France's centennial gift to the United States and a reminder of the French-American alliance during the revolutionary war.

born, in the late 1700s—the United States, France, and other nations opened the world's eyes to the necessity of legal rights for all citizens. An archives preserves, on paper then and in several formats today, the written or pictorial legal proof of the past, which no dictator or monarch can deny. Land claims,

In November 1982, the Gerald R. Ford Library in Ann Arbor, Michigan, hosted a conference on the presidency, Congress, and foreign policy. Attending the conference were (from left) former government officials Zbigniew Brzezinski, Alexander Haig, Dean Rusk, Gerald Ford, William Rogers, and Brent Scowcroft.

citizenship papers, court proceedings, patent certificates, military-service records—all of these items are the proof of an individual's service to or claims upon a government. To entrust them to a permanent and safe holding place, a national archives, is to ensure that person's legal place in society.

In many nations less fortunate than the United States the doors to the records are locked to the public; the keys are held by an unnamed official, if there is any key at all, and on occasion the written proof of the past is rewritten to suit the government's current needs. There have been attempts to conceal government actions in America, most notably in the Watergate affair and Richard Nixon's efforts to block the release of his White House tapes. But the Freedom of Information Act, strengthened by Congress in the 1970s in response to those actions, goes far toward ensuring free access to information for all citizens. The legal rights of a U.S. citizen are the broadest in the world, and the National Archives is one of the largest and best-organized archives in the world—that is no coincidence.

It may be a political impossibility to have a completely free and open society, or an archives that reflects that honesty, but the National Archives of the United States is one of the best instruments available for enshrining history and protecting the law. Those two functions are intertwined in a way well worth preserving.

The National Archives
and Records Administration

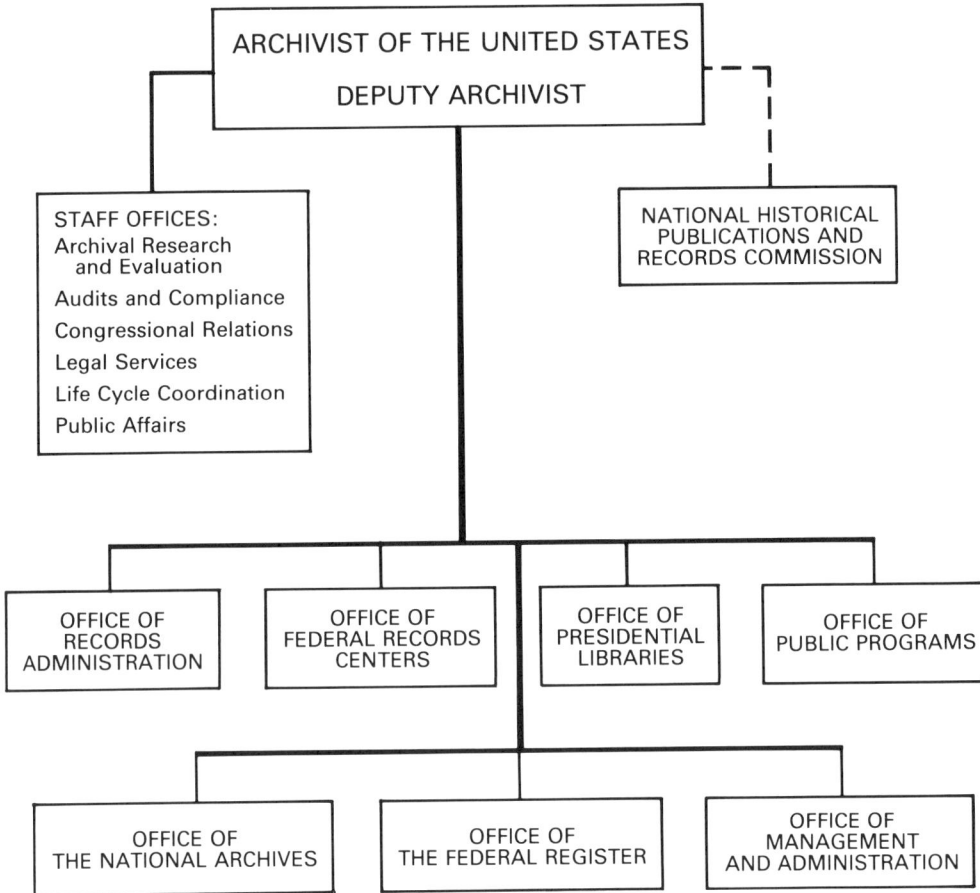

```
              ┌─────────────────────────────────┐ ┄ ┄ ┄ ┐
              │  ARCHIVIST OF THE UNITED STATES  │       ┊
              │                                  │       ┊
              │       DEPUTY ARCHIVIST           │       ┊
              └─────────────────────────────────┘       ┊
```

STAFF OFFICES:

Archival Research
 and Evaluation

Audits and Compliance

Congressional Relations

Legal Services

Life Cycle Coordination

Public Affairs

NATIONAL HISTORICAL
PUBLICATIONS AND
RECORDS COMMISSION

OFFICE OF
RECORDS
ADMINISTRATION

OFFICE OF
FEDERAL RECORDS
CENTERS

OFFICE OF
PRESIDENTIAL
LIBRARIES

OFFICE OF
PUBLIC PROGRAMS

OFFICE OF
THE NATIONAL ARCHIVES

OFFICE OF
THE FEDERAL REGISTER

OFFICE OF
MANAGEMENT
AND ADMINISTRATION

GLOSSARY

Charters of Freedom   The three documents—the Declaration of Independence, the Constitution, and the Bill of Rights—that are on permanent display in the rotunda of the National Archives building in Washington, D.C.

Declassification review   An appraisal made to determine whether a classified document may be released for public examination.

Electronic imaging system   An electronic camera and the body of data that it provides that are used to monitor a document's condition or to authenticate it by comparing it with a computer-coded photograph.

Federal Register   A daily publication that informs the public of changes and proposed changes in the rules and regulations of executive-branch agencies.

Finding aids   Guides prepared by archivists to help researchers use the Archives's records.

Microfilm   A film on which hundreds of pages of documents can be reproduced through a special photographic process.

Original order   An archival method that keeps records in the same order as the order in which they were created by their agency.

Primary source   An original document, letter, speech, or other piece of information.

Provenance   An archival method that files one organization's records separately from the records of any other organization.

Record group   A body of records filed as a unit by an archival agency, organized on the basis of related subject matter, date of creation, or some other unifying fact.

Secondary source   An article or book that uses an original document (a primary source) as the research basis for some or all of its claims.

SELECTED REFERENCES

Daniels, Maygene F., and Timothy Walch, eds. *A Modern Archives Reader: Basic Readings on Archives Theory and Practice.* Washington, DC: National Archives Trust Fund Board, 1984.

Gondos, Victor. *J. Franklin Jameson and the Birth of the National Archives, 1906–1926.* Philadelphia: University of Pennsylvania Press, 1981.

Jones, H. G. *The Records of a Nation.* New York: Atheneum, 1969.

McCoy, Donald R. *The National Archives: America's Ministry of Documents, 1934–1968.* Chapel Hill: University of North Carolina Press, 1978.

National Archives Trust Fund Board. *The American Image: Photographs from the National Archives, 1860–1960.* New York: Pantheon, 1979.

————. *Declaration of Independence: The Adventures of a Document.* Washington, DC: National Archives Trust Fund Board, 1976.

————. *Genealogical Research in the National Archives.* Washington, DC: National Archives Trust Fund Board, 1982.

————. *Milestone Documents in the National Archives.* Washington, DC: National Archives Trust Fund Board, 1986.

Prologue: Journal of the National Archives. National Archives Trust Fund Board, published quarterly.

Viola, Herman J. *The National Archives of the United States.* New York: Abrams, 1984.

Walch, Timothy, ed. *Guardian of Heritage: Essays on the History of the National Archives.* Washington, DC: National Archives Trust Fund Board, 1985.

INDEX

Christina Rudy Smith worked at the National Archives for 12 years, in the Office of Program Analysis and Improvement, the Office of Presidential Libraries, and as chief of the Exhibits Branch from 1984 to 1986. She holds a B.A. in English from American University and an M.A. in English literature from Stanford University. She has published articles in *Prologue: Journal of the National Archives* and *American Archivist* and has written for several government publications.

Arthur M. Schlesinger, jr., served in the White House as special assistant to Presidents Kennedy and Johnson. He is the author of numerous works in American history and has twice been awarded the Pulitzer Prize. He taught history at Harvard College for many years and is currently Albert Schweitzer Professor of the Humanities at the City College of New York.

PICTURE CREDITS